THE LAST BOOK OF HOMER

José Rivera

BROADWAY PLAY PUBLISHING INC
New York
www.broadwayplaypublishing.com
info@broadwayplaypublishing.com

THE LAST BOOK OF HOMER
© Copyright 2021 José Rivera

First edition: June 2021
I S B N: 978-0-88145-902-9

Book design: Marie Donovan
Page make-up: Adobe InDesign
Typeface: Palatino

THE LAST BOOK OF HOMER has been developed at the Victory Gardens Theater, New Works Brooklyn, Brooklyn College Department of Theater, Huntington Theatre Company, Atlantic Theater Company, Ensemble Studio Theatre, The Lark, The Alliance Theatre, The Center, Barnard College, New York Stage and Film, the New York Writing Group, and Torn Page with the following actors and artists:

Chay Yew, Isaac Gomez, Eddie Martinez, Marvin Quijada, Ricardo Gutierrez, Ramon Carmin, Miguel Nuñez, Jonathan Berry, Polly Hubbard, Jinni Pike, Mateo Hurtado, Jorge Chapa, José Joaquin Perez, Alfredo Narciso, Bobby Plasencia, Andy Buck, Marisela González, Sara Koviak, David Zayas, Felix Angel Solis, Paco Lozano-Weise, J W Cortez, Joél Pérez, Melinda Lopez, Diego Arciniegas, Gerardo Rodriguez, Salvatore Inzerillo, Carlo Alban, Armando Reisco, Frank Harts, Teddy Cañez, Adrian Martinez, Raúl Castillo.

CHARACTERS & SETTING

BUDDHA, *a Puerto Rican man, 40s, ex-Army*
WEASEL, *a Puerto Rican man, 40s, ex-Marine*
JOSEPH SMITH, *a Puerto Rican man, 40s, ex-Marine*
GOD, *a Puerto Rican man, 40s, ex-Army*

A small town motel in Central Mexico
Time: A few years ago

for Julio Rivera

ACT ONE

(June. A few years ago. 2:00 PM)

(A shitty motel room at the edge of a small, dusty town in Central Mexico)

(Windows with thread-bare curtains barely keep out the intense desert sunlight.)

(Sad motel art: scenes of Aztec glory. Stained carpeting that smells like too many bad nights. An old television on a glass table.)

(Several suitcases, backpacks, rolled up sleeping bags, bags of groceries, a cooler full of beer.)

(An old air conditioner hums and sputters, but the room is very hot.)

(Munching nervously from a box of Ritz Crackers, is Charlie, A K A BUDDHA, *a Puerto Rican of 47.)*

*(*BUDDHA *is a former Army sergeant, tall, strong, crowding 300 pounds, with huge hands, sharp eyes, a gentle face, goatee, deep voice and explosive laugh.)*

(Gregarious, charming, and playful, BUDDHA *is hard of hearing and speaks too loud. He lives with constant pain in his knees and he walks with a cane.)*

*(*BUDDHA *wears old combat boots, jeans and a black P O W remembrance T-shirt that says, "Some gave all. All gave some.")*

(His brother Hector, a.k.a. WEASEL, *a former Marine, 43, drinks a beer, squats on the floor, and peeks through the curtains with high-powered binoculars.)*

*(*WEASEL *is in good physical shape and looks younger than his age. He's got large, soulful eyes, very short hair, a moustache, a mischievous handsome smile.)*

(The youngest of six, there is still something of the irresponsible, irrepressible boy in WEASEL.*)*

*(*WEASEL *wears a black Harley-Davidson t-shirt, boots, jeans, and a grotesque devil tattooed on his shoulder.)*

(The door opens and their brother Julio, A K A JOSEPH SMITH, *49, in sunglasses, holding a small backpack, enters.)*

*(*JOSEPH SMITH *is short, well over 200 pounds, skin filled with old acne scars, short hair, dark bright eyes, moustache and goatee.)*

*(A former body builder and Marine—and now a Mormon—*JOSEPH SMITH *is complex, soft-spoken, witty, solemn, and the most anal and responsible of the brothers.)*

*(*JOSEPH SMITH *wears jeans, boots, and a black Boston Patriots T-shirt.)*

(The brothers have come a long way and none have slept or eaten in 30 hours. They've just driven 4 hours nonstop from Mexico City to be here.)

(They're exhausted, punchy, hungry, homesick and a little freaked out.)

BUDDHA: Where the fuck is God? I don't see God!

JOSEPH SMITH: Someone refrain me before I kill the little Nazi!

WEASEL: What happened? I don't see weapons!

*(*JOSEPH SMITH *angrily throws the backpack on a bed, addresses* BUDDHA.*)*

JOSEPH SMITH: You get that first aid like I told you? I got a forehead pain ready to burst through my face like *Alien.*

BUDDHA: In the bag.

JOSEPH SMITH: Where? Which bag? There are three bags!

BUDDHA: You think I'm gonna hand it to you like a fuckin' maid, you're on crack!

WEASEL: God already blow this shit like I been predicting?

JOSEPH SMITH: Little Nazi's on the phone to Janet of course.

BUDDHA: We said no spousal contact!

WEASEL: You think the rules apply to that douche nozzle?

(JOSEPH SMITH rummages through the bags of groceries.)

JOSEPH SMITH: Where's the aspirin, Buddha? Didn't you think to buy no aspirin?

BUDDHA: You didn't say "aspirin," you said "first aid."

JOSEPH SMITH: I said "first aid—and stuff."

BUDDHA: How was I supposed to know there wasn't gonna be aspirin in the fuckin' first aid?

JOSEPH SMITH: Think, Charlie! "Stuff" includes aspirin and stuff! That Aztec sun's butchering my eyes.

BUDDHA: If you grab your balls and get your eyes operated, like I been begging, maybe you could fuckin' see.

JOSEPH SMITH: My eyes are fine! I look around and I see Mexico!

(WEASEL goes to the door, calls out.)

WEASEL: Yo, Tony! You on your period or what?

JOSEPH SMITH: Don't yell out real names, shit bird!

WEASEL: You just said "Charlie!"

JOSEPH SMITH: Why don't you just tell the entire town we're here and stuff?

BUDDHA: I think the town knows.

WEASEL: How do they know? Who told them? Shit!

BUDDHA: We did! You see any North Americans out there? We might as well wear a T-shirt that says "Clueless Gringo".

WEASEL: Maybe you're the gringo, homeboy, but I'm pure Puerto Rican and at least I speak Spanish.

BUDDHA: I speak perfect Spanish! Coño tu madre! Me cago en los ojos y la kricka de Marta!

(BUDDHA *laughs. He loves to laugh, his laugh is explosive.*)

(JOSEPH SMITH *rummages through the grocery bags, tears into a bag of taco chips and beef jerky and eats ravenously. Looks warily at a wrapped sandwich and bottle of Mountain Dew.*)

JOSEPH SMITH: Really? Mountain Dew? You couldn't get no Dr Pepper?

BUDDHA: Well, ain't I got a permanent case of the dumb-asses today?

JOSEPH SMITH: And what's this? Horse cock sandwich, Charlie?

BUDDHA: Hey, it's *fuckin'* Buddha now, 'kay there, Joseph Smith?

JOSEPH SMITH: You say that name with some respect, boy.

WEASEL: I can't believe you're still a Mormon—

JOSEPH SMITH: Hey! I will always be a Mormon! And don't just think about yourself, okay Buddha? A fighting unit needs—

BUDDHA: *Fighting* unit? I'm throwing the bullshit flag on that one, my brother!

JOSEPH SMITH: —it needs *cohesion* and stuff, means everyone's got each other's back, even for little things like chow.

BUDDHA: "Cohesion!" You learn that from the Marines' Big Book of Words?

*(*JOSEPH SMITH *pulls a pineapple from a bag and laughs.)*

JOSEPH SMITH: Oh, Buddha. Priceless. A *pineapple.* That's practical. Ah, at least you remembered the grapes.
(He eats the grapes without washing them.)

BUDDHA: So where are the fuck are the fucking weapons? And where's God at?

JOSEPH SMITH: Now God wants to go Elvis on this mission.

BUDDHA: You assholes think I'm going in there hand-to-hand? Against them savage killers? I look that *stupid* to you? Don't answer that!

*(*WEASEL *opens the cooler, takes out a bottle of beer, opens it with the bottle opener on his ring.)*

WEASEL: I been saying God's unhinged, but no, I'm like the crazy dude on the street, spewing all kinds of truth, and mankind just waltzes on by, deaf and clueless…

JOSEPH SMITH: Man, you just got your mangina all in a state today, don't you?

WEASEL: I ain't got a mangina!

BUDDHA: Nothing's going to happen to your precious mangina, Weas'.

WEASEL: You can look me in my face and *guarantee*
I'm going to see Linda and Stevie again and not come
home missing an eye or a leg or half my fucking mind?

BUDDHA: What a pussy!

JOSEPH SMITH: God was going along just fine. Totally
rational. He had his list. He knew what he wanted. He
was talking in his indoor voice—"Yes sir, no sir." The
money is literally *in the bag*. I'm shaking on the inside
and he's cooler than a snowman. We're *this* close and
the dealer makes some lame-ass joke about America
losing the Vietnam War and Afghanistan.
And God's *eyes*, man—it's like I see this demon
erupting inside his mind! He pops off some racist shit
to the dealer how Mexicans don't have the cojones
to *fight* a war and how he banged the dude's mother
twice before the huevos rancheros this morning—and
fundamentally and completely kills the whole deal.

BUDDHA: You said he was stable enough to lead this
mission.

JOSEPH SMITH: We talked for hours last night.
Completely lucid.

WEASEL: Just try *suggesting* he sees a shrink and watch
what happens.

BUDDHA: And if he's gone Captain Queeg? You gonna
be head motherfucker in charge, Smith?

JOSEPH SMITH: But the little Nazi is infantry, he knows
how to do this shit better than the rest of us do.

WEASEL: We need to pack up and go—and at least we
tried—how many other guys would've gone this far?

BUDDHA: Run away! Run away! Weasel wants to run
away! Get back to the wifey before dinner is cold and
Fox News is over!

WEASEL: Hey, Linda was ready to go nuclear on my ass when I told her I was going to Mexico with you clowns!

BUDDHA: Surprised she let out the leash long enough to let you go. She hand you the pair of balls she keeps in her purse?

WEASEL: Linda was gonna jump on the plane with me. She's all, "I got better gear than all you all fat asses!"

BUDDHA: She's got a point. It's like how many pregnant men can fit in one motel?

WEASEL: We had a major eruption 'bout this whole clusterfuck, sucks ass when she cries like that...

BUDDHA: Don't tell me about no crying. I hate seeing Tommy cry, man. I go out to buy cigarettes, he's like, "when are you comin' home, Daddy?" Gets all panicky an' shit.

JOSEPH SMITH: Panicky you're gonna die the way you suck those things. You go to the doctor like I asked you? Get that cough X-rayed?

BUDDHA: My lungs are fine! I breathe and I smell Mexico!

WEASEL: Don't you know the thing about crazy people is they're a genius at not *looking* crazy?

BUDDHA: My exes perfected that shit to a science...

JOSEPH SMITH: Yeah, *this* close, and the price was decent and the dude had the whole package and stuff, and the shit looked good.

BUDDHA: AKs? Grenades?

JOSEPH SMITH: Glocks, gas masks, rounds, body armor—the whole nine.

WEASEL: We need every swinging dick we got out there.

JOSEPH SMITH: I think it's 'cause he doesn't want his wife to be a widow and his daughter to be an orphan.

BUDDHA: Tommy was crying his eyes out when I left him. You think I wanted to leave him like that?

JOSEPH SMITH: Crying is Tommy's default setting and that's your fault.

BUDDHA: I don't come home? That boy's life is *done.*

WEASEL: Multiply that by my family and Madre and Emily's and all the other people we're connected to.

JOSEPH SMITH: From the get, I could tell God didn't like the dealer's attitude and stuff.

BUDDHA: It could be our last day on earth and he's freaked over some junkie Aztec's *attitude?*

JOSEPH SMITH: Indoor voice, Chuckles! And stop crunching those crackers so loud! I got one nerve left and you're building a friggin' *condo* on it!

BUDDHA: I'M HUNGRY. I ain't had chow since Zero Dark Stupid! I'm a growing boy! In all directions!

JOSEPH SMITH: At least eat the crackers out of a bowl like a person. Why do you have to eat them out of a box like a goddamn man-child? Crumbs everywhere! Gross!
(He sweeps the crumbs off the bed.)

(BUDDHA laughs, eats.)

(WEASEL opens another beer.)

(JOSEPH SMITH's phone ring. The tone is Styx's "Come Sail Away." They look at his phone, apprehensive.)

JOSEPH SMITH: It's Madre.

BUDDHA: Aw, *scheisse!*

(JOSEPH SMITH answers. His tone of voice completely changes, he's solicitous and self-conscious.)

JOSEPH SMITH: Hey, Ma. Si, we're very good, Ma. Si, the beach is so warm, the water is so blue, and la señoritas are so caliente! Everything cool over there? You see the arroz con gandules I made for you? And I left your medicina out, all neat and organized. Make sure you tell Tommy if you need *anything*, okay? I don't want to hear que tu no esta comiendo muy bueno.

(WEASEL *cringes.*)

WEASEL: His Spanish makes me want to pull out my molars. Through my eyes.

JOSEPH SMITH: Well, we can't really talk now, Ma, we're waiting for our drinks and stuff. Si—they bring the mojitos right out to the beach, where we are right now, the water's so blue. Whoa, I see seals and otters! They look just like puppies! You know how much you love puppies!

(BUDDHA *laughs hard.*)

(JOSEPH SMITH *glares at* BUDDHA *who giggles to himself.*)

JOSEPH SMITH: Love you too, Ma, we promise to have a really good time and come home safe and sound.
(He turns the phone off.)

BUDDHA: You just lied to your motherfucking mother. You just lied to a living saint. I love it.

JOSEPH SMITH: And she wants me to text her a picture of the damn otters!

WEASEL: Julio, serious, when God called, he said there'd be six guys on this mission. If I knew two dickhead friends of his were gonna bail—and it'd be just us four?—I never would've come. And now he has me goin' in for the extraction with him! I have maximum risk up in here!

BUDDHA: There's fuckin' risk all over this scenario, you baby—

WEASEL: But I'm not a Nazi taking target practice every day in the backyard like him. I don't got His and Hers shotguns hiding under my bed in case the Zombie Apocalypse hits Fort Wayne, Indiana. I mean, why can't *I* be the sniper and *Buddha* goes in with God to do the thing?

BUDDHA: You think I can go in with God? With this knee? And Joseph Smith's almost fat as me! And he's got gout!

WEASEL: But I'm a better marksman than you, Charlie—

BUDDHA: The bullshit you tell! You're better than Numb Nuts at making shit up!

WEASEL: And how do I fight at close quarters if I never done it before?

BUDDHA: On the job training, brother! Same as the men!

(JOSEPH SMITH *nervously paces, barely listening to the others.*)

JOSEPH SMITH: Numerically speaking, we're looking at a major dog fuck without God. I mean, what's the Plan B, you guys, if God walks?

BUDDHA: Plan B? What's the fuckin' Plan A? Did I miss the Plan A?

WEASEL: All I wanna know, does Plan A have an exit strategy?

BUDDHA: You and God grab Numb Nuts and run outta there through the nearest fuckin' exit, that's the strategy!

JOSEPH SMITH: Okay, with or without God, we need to solidify the chain of command and secure the narrative. We go through the script over and over until it's second nature in your brains.

BUDDHA: Like riding a bike, bro, I don't forget.

JOSEPH SMITH: It needs to be memorized and written in stone. I'm not doing this with you jokers any other way.

BUDDHA: Meaning we're stupid?

JOSEPH SMITH: Meaning there can be no mistakes out there. Meaning if the cartel doesn't kill us first and they catch us instead, they're virtuosos of the fine art of pulling your balls off with rusted pliers and cauterizing your wounds with tequila and a blowtorch.

WEASEL: Meaning you got ADD an' shit. Or dyslexia or whatever you got.

BUDDHA: I'm a college fuckin' graduate you punk-ass, ignorant, little slut!

WEASEL: Yeah, getting your bachelor's at the age of fifty!

BUDDHA: I ain't even fifty! I'm only forty-seven!

JOSEPH SMITH: If God bails, I'm going to draw up a modified schedule of events and alter the job descriptions and we take it from there. Don't like it? Go home to Mama.

(WEASEL *drinks some more.*)

BUDDHA: No voting?

JOSEPH SMITH: The democracy? You left that behind when we crossed the border on the plane.

BUDDHA: What's this chain of command based on as if I didn't know?

JOSEPH SMITH: Age.

BUDDHA: How convenient for you!

WEASEL: That makes you first and me last. Typical!

BUDDHA: Poor Weasel, the house mouse.

WEASEL: I ain't no house mouse.

BUDDHA: You're the fuckin' house mouse.

WEASEL: Once a Marine always a Marine.

BUDDHA: Once a low-energy Marine recruiter.

WEASEL: I'm the only one in this family who can run a half-marathon, yo!

JOSEPH SMITH: Oh God, here comes the half-marathon…

BUDDHA: You remember that your wife and son hadda carry you over the finish line in your last race, right?

JOSEPH SMITH: I think you had blacked out by then, Weas'. And you were foaming clouds of foam at the mouth and stuff.

WEASEL: Hey, I seen you old ladies limping your ass off through the airport like—old ladies.

BUDDHA: I got a bad knee, it ain't my fault.

WEASEL: "And where did I get a bad knee?"

BUDDHA: And where did I *get* a bad knee?

BUDDHA, JOSEPH SMITH, WEASEL: In combat!

BUDDHA: You ever hear of combat? It's something actual men do.

JOSEPH SMITH: Look, Buddha, before you go out, I'll help you wrap 'em up again—cuz you're only as young as your knees, brother.

BUDDHA: Okay, sure. Thanks, man. Awesome.

WEASEL: You're only as young as who you're sleeping with.

JOSEPH SMITH: That makes Numb Nuts the youngest in the family! We need to get him back to the States before all the high school proms start up. He'd be pissed if he missed those.

(The brothers laugh and high five.)

BUDDHA: What an asshole for getting himself into this. Don't he read the papers or watch the news? The drug war and shit?

JOSEPH SMITH: We just have to do this and do it fast and no mistakes and get him out of that hell-hole.

(Beat)

WEASEL: You think they're torturing him?

(Beat)

JOSEPH SMITH: Yeah, they're breaking his pencils. "No please, don't break my pencils! I need them to make up my stupid stories! My movies no one ever watches!"

BUDDHA: Snap!

JOSEPH SMITH: "Oh shit, my pencils, my precious pencils!"

BUDDHA: "We're gonna give you terrible reviews!"

JOSEPH SMITH: "Fuck you, I already got those!"

BUDDHA: "We're gonna tell everyone your real age!"

JOSEPH SMITH: "*Barbarians!* They have a Geneva Convention for that shit!"

(BUDDHA and JOSEPH SMITH laugh, high five, bump fists. In the uneasy silence that follows ...)

WEASEL: Geneva Convention don't cover what those people are. Their evil's on a whole other stratosphere. There ain't no one gonna protect our brother in that room. It's gonna be just him and all the pain they make him feel...

(The others think about the unthinkable reality of this in silence.)

(Suddenly the door opens and Tony, A K A GOD, *45, pulling a small rolling suitcase, comes in.)*

(GOD *is a decorated ex-Army sergeant, blond with intense blue-eyes, handsome, relatively trim, hot-headed, out-spoken, and blunt, a natural leader with the instincts of a true warrior.*)

(GOD *wears jeans and a black Victory Motorcycle T-shirt and is the only one without facial hair. Like the others, he hasn't slept in 30 hours.*)

(*His presence in the room has an immediate sobering and focusing effect on the others.*)

(*As* GOD *enters,* BUDDHA *laughs with relief and grabs him in a big, energetic bear hug.*)

BUDDHA: Whaddup buttercup!?

GOD: Dude, who picked this place? It smells like fourteen kinds of urine and vomit in here.

BUDDHA: Actually it's come.

GOD: Someone better explain to Joseph Smith what that is!

(WEASEL, *a little tipsy, laughs, swigs a beer, and sings—*)

WEASEL: "Like a Virgin! Like a Vir-ir-irgin!"

JOSEPH SMITH: I am not a virgin!

(GOD *gives* WEASEL *a dark look.*)

GOD: She's *drinking*? She can't be drinking at her post!

BUDDHA: Okay, man, so what's your status?

WEASEL: Eat me, God. I don't care.

BUDDHA: So you done being crazy? Or you *temporarily* sane?

GOD: Look, it's complicated, alright?

JOSEPH SMITH: There isn't any time for complicated, son.

WEASEL: Yeah they already broke his pencils.

GOD: What pencils? Weasel stop fucking drinking!

(WEASEL *throws the beer can away and gets in* GOD'*s face.*)

WEASEL: Hey, you don't waltz in here after you choked trying to recruit two men and then compromised everything with your little hissy-fit—

GOD: What kind of man uses the word "hissy-fit?"

BUDDHA: 'Cause now that we lost your two guys, the mission requires four—count 'em—*four men.* You bail on us, and we got ourselves nothing but a bag of dicks out here.

JOSEPH SMITH: And you can tell Madre why you didn't try to save her oldest son. That she supposedly loves more than the rest of us.

BUDDHA: And tell Lucy why you didn't rescue her old man.

WEASEL: And explain to Maritza why her daddy's a born pussy.

GOD: *I am just going to monkey stomp you, Weas'*—!

(*With lightning speed, God grabs Weasel, puts him in a head-lock and forces him to the ground. They trade punches—knock over furniture, break lamps.*)

(JOSEPH SMITH *and* BUDDHA *pull* GOD *and* WEASEL *apart.*)

JOSEPH SMITH: Settle down, that's an order, both of you!

(WEASEL *and* GOD *retreat to opposite sides of the room. God glares at* WEASEL.*)

GOD: You got lucky right now. Savor the feeling, chump.

(WEASEL *gives* GOD *the finger, rubs his sore neck.*)

JOSEPH SMITH: Your neck okay, Hector? You need me to look at it?

WEASEL: I'M FUCKING FUCKING PEACHY!

(He opens another beer.)

(JOSEPH SMITH puts his arm around GOD.)

JOSEPH SMITH: Look, man, I know. Okay? We're all in the same boat with you. Maritza is three. I get it. Janet wants you home. I get that too.

GOD: Jan keeps saying it's a job for trained military or the Mexican police or the U S Embassy.

BUDDHA: I don't know about you, but underneath the layers of beer flab and busted knee joints, I'm still trained military.

WEASEL: Me too.

BUDDHA: Girl Scouts ain't military, sistah! Though I know you like the little uniforms and camp songs!

JOSEPH SMITH: The Mexican police would never come near those cold-blooded killers. Not for some stupid American liberal geek who had his ass captured shooting a movie about Greeks and Trojans!

BUDDHA: The Embassy's a joke when it comes to kidnapped Americans.

JOSEPH SMITH: And you were ready to burn half the Yucatan to get Numb Nuts back when you saw the video, Ton'. You saw what your duty was and you decided to do it. I don't know what changed.

(Beat)

GOD: Maritza hugged me good-bye. At the airport. And I had to lie to her face. And I didn't like thinking those could be my last words to her.

JOSEPH SMITH: We all sacrificed. Buddha left Tommy. Weasel left Linda and Stevie.

BUDDHA: Joseph Smith ain't left nobody 'cause he's still ain't popped his cherry…

JOSEPH SMITH: I left a job I'd like to keep in this
economy. And an eighty-two year-old Madre who's all
alone with a nine-year-old boy waiting for us to come
home, and all of us here have jobs.

WEASEL: Well, except for Buddha...

BUDDHA: I got like seventeen applications out there
and it's a recession in New Hampshire. I could get a
call tomorrow for work. But no! I'm in fuckin Mexico
with the Little Rascals!

WEASEL: Yeah! Julio is Spanky! No, Darla!

JOSEPH SMITH: Everyone's life is now totally on hold
until we finish this. And we agreed that all risk
would be shared equally—as well as all the pain.
That's what we committed to before we got on those
planes. Because we have to do this. Because there is no
choice in the matter. Numb Nuts is in a major league
clusterfuck and there is no choice.

BUDDHA: And Lucy will throw some killer-santeria-
mojo at us if we go home without him.

GOD: But look at us. Former military glory. Decorated
vets—well except for Weasel here, of course—

BUDDHA: Hec', don't even try to tell us that airplane
story again—

WEASEL: I don't know why you guys don't believe me!
I have the papers! From Congress!

GOD: Over-weight, bad knees and backs, asthma,
cataracts, gout, P T S D bordering on dementia and
none of us limp dicks can fuckin' hear.

BUDDHA: What'd he say?

(WEASEL *laughs mockingly at* BUDDHA's *lame joke.*)

WEASEL: He said "what'd he say?" after God say none
of us can hear!—that's comedy gold, yo!

(BUDDHA *makes a mock-threatening gesture at Weasel and God rolls his eyes.*)

GOD: And none of us have fired a weapon in combat in forever. It's a fucked situation all around.

JOSEPH SMITH: But it's our big brother, Ton'.

GOD: Like I don't know?

JOSEPH SMITH: And the plan is a workable plan. Which you and I designed to perfection.

GOD: Okay, I know!

JOSEPH SMITH: And you don't abandon a fellow soldier on the field of combat.

WEASEL: And "fellow soldier" applies to Numb Nuts—how?

BUDDHA: Being our brother makes him an honorary grunt!

WEASEL: Oh, we abandoned reality long ago and far away with that shit!

JOSEPH SMITH: The only thing those pukes know is guerilla-style warfare. They're not prepared for a classic military-designed assault like we have. They don't know who we are and they don't expect us. That's the magic of it. And sure we're a little rusty. But God you got more decoration than the Mall of America on Christmas for all the Claude Van Damme shit you pulled overseas.

GOD: A millenium ago—

JOSEPH SMITH: Buddha's still an animal with his strength and lightning with his hands. I lost twenty pounds since Christmas. And Weasel. Weasel is. Weasel runs half-marathons, yo!

(WEASEL *throws himself on the bed, buries his head under a pillow.*)

(GOD *is deep in thought, wavering.*)

BUDDHA: You know what you hate about this, little brother?

GOD: Oh Buddha, please, reach into your vast storehouse of knowledge and wisdom acquired from Loony Tunes episodes—

BUDDHA: Hello? Classics!

GOD: —and enlighten me on what exactly I hate about this.

BUDDHA: It's a matter of honor. Of our family. Of our father who would've been already in that fucking building saving his oldest son. The honor of a promise. The honor that we never ignore a challenge. And the fact that you can't turn your back on honor. Ever.

(GOD *is silent…this is an argument that effects him deeply, whether he would admit it or not.*)

GOD: Whatever, Freud.

JOSEPH SMITH: Decision, Ton'. Clock's counting to zero.

GOD: I hate each of you pukes.

(WEASEL *gets out of bed, goes to open another beer.*)

WEASEL: Don't lump me in with these losers. I happen to have a son going to graduate from high school this year and I sure would love to be alive to see that shit. And next year Linda's going to be head of the music department. And that comes with a nice raise because they totally love her at that school. Man, I'm so proud of her. It's cool seeing how people respect her. And now, financially, we can finally do shit we always wanted. I'm paying debts. Repairing the house and fixing the Scout. Life is finally where it should be and she really…is…and weren't you saving up to buy a Harley, Julio…is…is anybody *listening* to me?

(JOSEPH SMITH *and* BUDDHA *ignore* WEASEL *and focus on* GOD, *who is uneasy, deep in thought.*)

JOSEPH SMITH: If either Numb Nuts or Lucy is ever in any serious trouble, in any part of the world, they're in jail or kidnapped or sick and dying, we promised that we'd be there in twenty-four hours or less to take care of them. That was our wedding present to them. From all four of us.

GOD: This is why you don't make promises at a wedding when your brain is soaked in mojitos.

JOSEPH SMITH: Now we got a chance to redeem the promise. To show them that we meant it. That we're still warriors. That we're not useless old men. That some people in this jaded, dishonest world *actually keep their word.*

(This silences the brothers a moment.)

WEASEL: Yeah but why didn't we think to make a fucking exception for Mexican drug cartels?

BUDDHA: You three could be fucking exempted from this promise if you want. But I'll fuckin' go in that hell-pit by myself if I have to. Can I make that more clearer? I don't need none of you girls to finish this, I swear, bum leg, bum hearing, a hundred extra pounds, whatever, but I ain't leaving Mexico without my brother either sittin' next to me hitting on the flight attendants, or in a fuckin' wooden box in cargo. Either way, I swear, I will go alone and that's my last word on this, so fuck y'all.

(The others take this in silently.)

(JOSEPH SMITH *goes to* BUDDHA *and puts an arm around his shoulders.*)

JOSEPH SMITH: You're not going into anything alone as long as I'm around breathing and walking, brother, okay?

(BUDDHA *kisses* JOSEPH SMITH *on the cheek.*)

BUDDHA: That's the loyalty shit I'm talking about.

(BUDDHA *and* JOSEPH SMITH *embrace.*)

(GOD *pretends to vomit.*)

(JOSEPH SMITH *takes out his cellphone.*)

GOD: Who the fuck are you calling?

(JOSEPH SMITH *hits a number, looking right at* GOD.)

JOSEPH SMITH: Yo, Emily? It's your favorite brother.

GOD: Fuck, no, that just isn't fair…

JOSEPH SMITH: Settle down, Em', I can't understand—no, we don't have him yet! EMILY! Yeah we all arrived here okay and stuff. Well, it's not going so great. The first meeting to buy arms fell apart over logistical bullcrap—*Emmy, c'mon!* It's going to be okay. We're going to rescue him. Look, God—that's Tony's call sign—God has something important he needs to tell you.

(JOSEPH SMITH *goes to hand* GOD *the cellphone.*)

(GOD *runs to the other side of the room.*)

(BUDDHA *sneaks up behind* GOD, *grabs him.* GOD *and* BUDDHA *struggle.*)

(GOD *tries to slam* BUDDHA *backward into a wall—hits a window. Glass goes flying.*)

GOD: You bitches are so gonna need to meet Jesus!

(WEASEL *goes to the window, looks out.*)

WEASEL: Hola! Cómo están? No se preocupen, todo bien!

(JOSEPH SMITH, *completely unfazed by the mayhem, speaks to the phone.*)

JOSEPH SMITH: Emily, he's right here. He has the current status on our plans and stuff.

(GOD *struggles as Joseph Smith approaches him with the phone.*)

(WEASEL *shakes his head, picks up glass from the floor. Keeps sneaking drinks.*)

(JOSEPH SMITH *puts the phone to* GOD's *ear.* GOD *realizes it's hopeless to struggle against* BUDDHA *and stops.*)

(BUDDHA *lets him go.* GOD *takes the phone.*)

GOD: Yeah, hi, Em. Yeah, I'm okay. Yeah we're situated across the street from the cartel. Yeah, we got the Gonzales's money. Yeah, I know his life's in—yeah, I *know*, Em. Yeah, I miss him too and I don't want— yeah, it's an injustice and evil should not be allowed to—yeah, of course I *love him!* I never said I didn't love him! No, I'm not scared! Do I look scared?!
(Beat. He listens unable to resist his sister's passionate arguments.)
You're right. Okay. Fine.
(Beat. He takes a long breath.)
What we're going to do. We're going to. We're going to try again. With another dealer. Get the weapons to finish this shit-show, then going in with hellfire and make those pukes feel the pain. And he's going to come out without a scratch on his pretty little ass. I CAN BE SARCASTIC IF I WANT. Yes, that's a promise, Emily. He's coming home. On Mom's eyes, it's a promise. Love you too, baby, hang in there.

(GOD *hands the phone back to* JOSEPH SMITH. JOSEPH SMITH *smiles, grabs* GOD *and embraces him.*)

JOSEPH SMITH: He mans up and everything!

WEASEL: Wow, one word from Emily and you shit yourself.

JOSEPH SMITH: Nothing in this world scares this boy like his big sister!

BUDDHA: Just *knew* you couldn't turn your back, man, we a fighting unit *now* motherfuckas!

(BUDDHA *grabs* GOD *and* JOSEPH SMITH *and joins the embrace.*)

(WEASEL *stands apart.*)

BUDDHA: You too, house-mouse…

(BUDDHA *grabs Weasel and pulls him into the group embrace.*)

(*The embrace is long and deeply felt and is followed by kisses and back pounding.*)

(*Moments of silence follow as each of the brothers let this reality sink into them. They've reached the point of no return and they know it.*)

GOD: Yeah, well, don't get too fuckin' excited. If this isn't done to *perfection*, I still think it's suicide…

(WEASEL *cleans up the broken glass.*)

WEASEL: So we're not going home.

BUDDHA: You're stuck in Mexico with us, chump. So shut up and embrace the suck.

JOSEPH SMITH: By this time tomorrow. You'll be back on the block. And everything is cool. And you're a hero like you always wanted to be. And Numb Nuts pays major reparations and stuff.

BUDDHA: I'm totally keeping a list of expenses.

JOSEPH SMITH: Plus time away from work. Plus pain and suffering.

GOD: You're going charge him for the Mexican whorehouse too, Chucky?

BUDDHA: Just the spanking sessions.

GOD: He better write a movie about us after this. Ryan Gosling is me! The Rock is Buddha! Selena Gomez can play you, Hec'.

BUDDHA: He totally needs to get Shakira to belly-dance on my face at the after-party.

JOSEPH SMITH: I hear she only dates within her species, bro.

BUDDHA: Being the right species has always been beside the point with me!

WEASEL: It's true, I met his exes.

GOD: I swear on la kricka de Marta, the first thing we do, if we don't die and get through this, is KILL Numb Nuts.

(BUDDHA *laughs. He and* WEASEL *high five.* WEASEL *sneaks a drink.*)

BUDDHA: Yeah he ain't known torture 'till we get our hands on his dumb, liberal ass. Sorry— "progressive"!

GOD: And speaking of exes, I'm not looking forward to telling Janet I'm not coming home. You don't know the wrath of that woman.

JOSEPH SMITH: You don't have to tell your wife everything.

GOD: "You don't have to tell your wife everything." Dude, this is why you don't have a woman this whole decade.

BUDDHA: Or any decade.

JOSEPH SMITH: "Or any decade!" Oh, the comic relief is overwhelming! Just let's *do* this. We now, officially, have not a lot of time left on the meter and we still need to find a dealer and acquire the weaponry and drill the Plan A narrative.

(GOD *reluctantly opens his suitcase and pulls out a computer.*)

GOD: I have a list of cartels from the Spook on my computer. Phone numbers and addresses. We just go down the list.

WEASEL: How come the Spook don't supply the arms?

BUDDHA: 'Cause maybe he don't wanna lose his job at the Bureau?

GOD: Let's fuckin' break it down. My fucking headache is epic. Any more of those beers?

BUDDHA: Now you're talking like a goddamn Iglesia, brother!

(BUDDHA *opens the cooler and tosses* GOD *a beer.*)

(JOSEPH SMITH *lies on the floor.*)

(GOD *gives him a look and half-smile.*)

GOD: And you're doing what?

JOSEPH SMITH: Trying a sit-up.
(*He tries hard to do a sit up and can't. He laughs.*)
Okay I tried it.
(*It takes a while for him to get back on his feet. He wheezes.*)

(BUDDHA *takes* WEASEL's *binoculars, goes to the windows, peeks out from behind the curtains.*)

GOD: Yo, Rain Man. What the fuck?

BUDDHA: Checking out their look-out guy on the roof.

GOD: You know he probably hasn't changed positions since we got here.

WEASEL: So the Spook is *totally* sure that's where they're keeping him? That house over there? Across the street? With the gates on the windows? And the razor wire? And the salivating pits?

BUDDHA: That be the one, girlfriend!

WEASEL: But what if we're attacking the wrong gang?

BUDDHA: There's two vatos pulling guard duty. There was one before.

(GOD *smacks the computer.*)

GOD: Stupid fucking wireless, *get me connected, puta!*

(*Ignored,* WEASEL *looks around, incredulous.*)

WEASEL: Okay, I didn't just ask the kind of question that means the difference between victory and massacre…

BUDDHA: They got automatics.

GOD: They probably have binoculars too, which means they're looking at us fuckin' looking at them. Man, *tankers!*

BUDDHA: What, "tankers"? Tankers were the only ones who fuckin' did any real combat in Desert Storm.

GOD: Shooting at each other!

BUDDHA: And runnin' over crunchies like you!

JOSEPH SMITH: I love how you Army guys have those sophisticated warnings. "Danger, close!"

GOD: Yeah, us Army guys. The ones that sweep in to annihilate the enemy, so you little jar heads can show up when the bullets stop flying—and serve us lunch.

JOSEPH SMITH: U S M C. "First to Fight", brother. Right, Weasel?

WEASEL: Oorah. First to fight.

GOD: U S M C. Uncle Sam's Misguided Children. Uncomplicated Shit Made Complicated.

BUDDHA: I'm looking for patterns. See if they're shifts.

JOSEPH SMITH: Of course there's shifts. You think one guy's going to stay up there twenty-four seven? Even gangstas have to pee.

BUDDHA: Think they're wearing body armor.

GOD: Of course they are. They're fuckin' fighting an insurgency every day of the week.

BUDDHA: Gonna have to shoot them in the head, that's a smaller target.

(WEASEL *checks his watch.*)

WEASEL: I'm totally missing Linda's recital. Her kids are doing songs from *The Fantasticks.* Whatever that is. Did I tell you she got a promotion?

(*No response from the others.*)

GOD: I GOT IT! Aw, fuck, I just lost it! Coño tu madre!

(BUDDHA *scans the town with his binoculars.*)

JOSEPH SMITH: Checking out the skirts, buddy?

BUDDHA: Man, it's just the saddest fuckin' place. The kids look dusty on the *inside,* like from swallowing chunks of desert their whole life.

JOSEPH SMITH: Kills me to see kids that way.

BUDDHA: Yeah, even little ones got old man faces and zonked-out eyes cuzza seeing too much panic and sunlight. Their skin's pulled so tight over their faces, they can't make a human smile…

JOSEPH SMITH: Try living in a combat zone since the day you're born. See how much you laugh.

BUDDHA: Fuckin' cartels! Like they're God and got rights to kill, take everything they got. Make every hour a horror movie. The cops? Scared shitless and bought and mortgaged. So, for real, we're *liberators* of this town! We're gonna get a monument—and novias! (*He laughs.*)

GOD: Wasn't there some chick Numb Nuts was going to set you up with?

BUDDHA: Met her at the screening of his movie.

GOD: You're going to go for ex-wife number three?

WEASEL: How much alimony can one guy pay?

JOSEPH SMITH: But the dude could use the sex-ercize…

BUDDHA: But this girl is the finest thing. And I am fuckin' *gone* the minute I see her, I'm thinking "out of your league, negro," but before I know it, Numb Nuts is bringing her over to me and we say hi and she has a smile that brings the dead to life, the tightest, little booty, and she's totally into my war stories and don't give a fuck 'bout my bad knee, and my son, and P T S D, and screeching nightmares, and two ex-wives with their fuckin' venom still in me, and numbness in my right hand, and muffled hearing, and mood swings, and smoker's cough, and a few extra tons, and uncontrollable twitching in my fa-fa-fa-face! She and me exchange jokes and recipes and emails. We been talking about getting dinner if I can make it to the city next month. If I get back alive.

JOSEPH SMITH: She a hooker?

BUDDHA: A filmmaker, asshole.

WEASEL: I guess that's the same thing.

(GOD *bangs the computer against the bed.*)

GOD: GOD GIVE ME PATIENCE WITH THIS PINCHE INTERNET!

(JOSEPH SMITH *laughs.*)

JOSEPH SMITH: You've been in Mexico too long, cabrón!

BUDDHA: Orale, carnal! Chingao, esse!

(GOD, JOSEPH SMITH, *and* BUDDHA *laugh.*)

(WEASEL *groans, sneaks another beer. He is tipsier than ever and staggers to* GOD.)

WEASEL: Yo, Ton'. You know I have no real fucking clue what's going on in your life? Except what Numb

Nuts and Emily tell me—you quit Ratheon and all that
bread to teach eighth grade history in the inner city?
That true?

(GOD *has to walk away from his computer or he's going to
hurl it through a window.*)

GOD: Didn't feel like making bombs my whole life,
okay?

JOSEPH SMITH: Eighth grade is a killer age.

(GOD *lights a cigarette, paces nervously.*)

GOD: Like half the boys have no fathers around, being
raised by grandma. They uhm. *Fuck, it's so fucked up...*
(*His eyes suddenly, unexpectedly, moisten up and he looks
away.*)

JOSEPH SMITH: Wait. Are you having *feelings*?

BUDDHA: Dios mio, I gotta post this!

GOD: Ha ha. They look at me sometimes, these almost-
men, their *eyes*. Like bullets, you know? They fucking
shred me with all the things they don't have. So I take
them bowling, sometimes to the E R. Buy pizza for
the class, and milk, give them old pens and books, or
cookies, or socks. Or we go to the Salvation Army for
sneakers and a coat and a heart-to-heart about girls or
God or jobs or rap songs or death.

(*The others take this in silently.*)

GOD: I could work twenty-four seven and I'll still never
give them, you know, that one, unreplaceable fucking
thing they could get from a father. I just don't have the
power in me. Fuck it, man! Why the fuck am I talking
about this? We gots work to do, bitches!

WEASEL: Respect the hell out of that...

BUDDHA: Fuckin' fierce, Ton'...

(GOD *ignores them and goes back to his computer. Bangs on it hard. And suddenly gets the internet to work.)*

GOD: WHAT?! *Yes!* THERE IS A CHRIST! Okay! Lets review. Here's the video the motherfuckers sent to Lucy Saturday at 21:00, New York time, day they took him, the one Lucy sent me and Joseph Smith. He doesn't look too bad.

(BUDDHA, GOD, JOSEPH SMITH, *and* WEASEL *crowd around the computer and watch in silence.)*

WEASEL: That's the look of a terrified man...

GOD: The Spook says the location for the movie was supposed to be locked down tight. So he thinks it was an inside job. Says it's a new upstart group, a splinter group, young guys, a little crazy he said, maybe like ten of them vatos at the most. Out to prove themselves by taking a high profile international target—but the best they could get was Numb Nuts. But they might also have a whole room of hostages in the hideout. Local corporate types and cake eaters, officers in the other cartels, cops, sex slaves and shit.

BUDDHA: If they got children in there, *fuck...*

JOSEPH SMITH: A lot of women and girls have been disappeared from this area, too. Like in the thousands.

GOD: The González's wired the money, then the enemy sent a second video you guys haven't seen. Lucy sent it this morning. Numb Nuts the Sequel. Brace yourselves. It's grim.

(GOD *downloads the second video. The brothers are silent as they watch.)*

WEASEL: Both eyes are black.

BUDDHA: Can't hardly sit up.

GOD: Yesterday morning, Tuesday at 8:00, local time. If Lucy's parents don't make the next ransom...

WEASEL: How much time they say?

GOD: In the original demand, twenty-four hours—in the second, thirty-six. If they stick to that timetable, the González family either coughs it up by sunset *tonight*—or we go in there *first*—or the cartel's going to systematically extract fingers and teeth and ears and gonads from our big brother without the benefit of anesthesia.

WEASEL: Fuck me.

GOD: González's already paid a hundred K. The goons upped it to two-fifty. An ice cold quarter mil.

WEASEL: González's got that kind of cash?

GOD: Lucy says they're tapped out with the first demand. They're going to have to borrow. But now the enemy thinks the González family's a walking A T M and they're not going to stop until Numb Nuts literally runs out of appendages and pints of blood.

WEASEL: He shit his pants.

JOSEPH SMITH: Those Pablo Escobars just qualified for extinction.

BUDDHA: Click that shit off, man.

(He goes to a corner of the room and does his best to make sure the others don't hear him weeping or wiping his eyes.)

(The others silently notice, they give him his space, don't say anything.)

JOSEPH SMITH: We're lucky, okay? These cartels hate each other and getting them to arm us is a no-brainer. As far as they know, we're doing their dirty work for them.

(GOD indicates his computer.)

GOD: The list of cartels from the Spook. Four majors and twenty other players.

BUDDHA: We gotta find a cartel, contact it, arrange
a meeting, travel, meet, haggle for the goods, test
the goods, pay them, get back here, get the vehicles
ready, get the sighting done and target practice, get
me situated in the hills, and go in for the deed—*all by
sunset?*

WEASEL: No one ever told me the shopping list. But
that's cool, I'm only going in there like I'm impervious
to pain and death.

GOD: Don't wet yourself.

(Reads from a list.)

AK-47s or M4s for you and me, Weas'. 30-round
clips. Six or eight clips each should do us sweet. Fifty-
caliber sniper rifle for the Buddha man. A Browning,
hopefully. With a box of 100 rounds. Nine-millimeter
Berettas. Or Glocks, if they have them. Seventeen
rounds a clip, so we need three clips. Forty-millimeter
grenade launcher for Joseph Smith with ten to fifteen
rounds. Frag, percussion, and smoke grenades. Gas
masks for you and me, Weasel. Oh and body armor all
around.

BUDDHA: Extra large model for moi!

*(JOSEPH SMITH unzips his small backpack. He inspects the
cash. The brothers stare at all that money.)*

JOSEPH SMITH: Thank you Dr González.

BUDDHA: Is it too late to say fuck it and fly to Vegas?

WEASEL: I'm so down, my brother!

GOD: I suggest Weasel and Buddha go up in the hills
west of the hideout and find a spot for Buddha to sight
the sniper rifle and effectively shoot from.

BUDDHA: 'Bout half a mile?

GOD: No more than that. Unless you're real confident
with your eyes.

JOSEPH SMITH: Make sure you've got lots of natural cover, Buddha. If they see you, we are absolutely and completely screwed.

BUDDHA: I'm a combat vet, remember?

JOSEPH SMITH: But this time you're not surrounded by tons of tank armor. You can't be visible or vulnerable out there.

BUDDHA: I said I fuckin' got it, Smith.

JOSEPH SMITH: Cover fire is *essential* for this to work—

BUDDHA: Will you stop telling me what I already fuckin' know?

JOSEPH SMITH: And it has to be high up, with the sun to your back.

BUDDHA: Well it can't be too high up 'cause of my knee.

GOD: We can't be worrying about your knee, Chuck, I'm sorry, it has to be pretty high, that's the best angle.

JOSEPH SMITH: You can do this, right?

BUDDHA: I can do this! I can do this! All of you can just "at ease" that shit!

GOD: Then after that, you guys take the truck and test out the best escape routes. We need to fuckin' *fly* out of here.

JOSEPH SMITH: While you guys are doing that, God and I will negotiate for arms and this time, dipshit, do *not* antagonize the man by telling him how you did the horizontal rumba with his mama this morning, okay? Buddha, you tested out that bike?

BUDDHA: I told you four times I did. You need to clean the shit out of your ears.

JOSEPH SMITH: Why are you sulking?

BUDDHA: 'Cause you're always shitting on me! Like I'm dumb as a box of rocks!

GOD: Ladies! Here's the Plan A script again. Memorize it or tattoo it to your butthole. Buddha's our guardian angel. He's going to be perched a half-mile away, high in the western hills with the sun setting to his back, with the Kawasaki and a high power sniper rifle. From there he will provide cover for Joe Smith who is going to launch grenades into the cartel's oil and gas depots from behind the latrine in the park across the street from the hideout.

WEASEL: If his eyes ain't killing him and he can see the target...

GOD: The depot will go up in massive mushroom cloud fireballs creating a diversion and bringing the drug dealing motherfuckers out of their nest...

BUDDHA: And meanwhile I'm picking 'em off the perimeter one by one.

WEASEL: Please no civilian casualties!

BUDDHA: I'm totally gettin' it on—bam! bam! bam!

GOD: Then Joseph Smith is on the Virago immediately getting his fat ass the fuck out of there and going to the truck.

BUDDHA: And they don't know where the fuck I'm firing from! This shit is fun!

GOD: In all the chaos, Weas' and I sneak to the side of the hideout and pitch grenades and smoke bombs into the window. If there are any maggots still inside, they run out, choking to death, dying. Then Weas' and I kick the door down, spray the room with bullets, and run in for the extraction. Done.

WEASEL: But we don't know what room he's in.

GOD: We don't know what room he's in.

WEASEL: So how do we find him?

GOD: We call out his name.

WEASEL: Oh, we just walk in and call out his name.

GOD: "Yo, Numb Nuts, where the fuck are you? Do you want to go home or what?"

WEASEL: So what if the room we toss the grenades in is the room where they have Numb Nuts?

GOD: Then he's probably dead and the party's over.

WEASEL: What if they have him handcuffed to a radiator? What if he's wounded and can't walk? What if there are twenty kidnapped orphan children named Pablo and Rosita in there too?

GOD: Then it gets complicated!

WEASEL: And no one's shooting at us this whole time?

GOD: Everyone's shooting at us, dude! That's why we have the body armor and we're tossing smoke and shooting first.

JOSEPH SMITH: Meanwhile, I ride to the truck, ditch the bike, and meet you guys outside the hideout entrance under Buddha's cover fire.

GOD: Along with civilians, Chuck, *don't shoot your brothers!*

BUDDHA: One dead little king-pin! Two dead little king-pins! Three dead little king-pins!

WEASEL: If your weapon don't jam. Or one of them don't pick you off first. Or you don't miss.

BUDDHA: I don't miss!

GOD: Me and Weasel grab the package and whoever else they have stashed in there, shoot our way to the street and pile everyone in the truck. Joseph Smith drives, I attend to the wounded and beat the living shit out of the package, and Weasel you're in the back firing in case anyone's chasing us. Though all ten should be dead by then. In two minutes we rendezvous with Buddha at the crossroads by the church on the north side of town.

BUDDHA: Then we drop Numb Nuts off at the Rio Grande and make the peckerhead swim home! That's one hell of a good script!

JOSEPH SMITH: Clean. Simple. Classic.

BUDDHA: Hells yeah, what could *possibly* go wrong?

(JOSEPH SMITH'*s phone rings. "Come Sail Away." He grabs his phone and looks at the incoming number.*)

JOSEPH SMITH: Who wants to update Lucy on how we're two men short, have no weapons, we're an hour behind schedule and still dicking the time away?

(*No one does. It's like the phone is radioactive.* GOD *grabs* JOSEPH SMITH'*s phone.*)

GOD: A band of pussies! Buddha, take my phone, try not to break it, and start calling bad guys—numbers are on the screen.

(GOD *hands his phone to* BUDDHA.)

BUDDHA: I don't break shit.

GOD, JOSEPH SMITH, WEASEL: You break shit.

GOD: Yo, Luc', how you doin' girl? It's your favorite brother-in-law!
(*Lighting a cigarette, he walks out the motel room with the phone.*)

(BUDDHA *looks at the numbers on* GOD'*s computer, punches them into* GOD'*s phone. Lighting a cigarette, he goes outside.*)

(WEASEL *goes to* JOSEPH SMITH.)

WEASEL: Julio, I can't go in with God for the extraction.

JOSEPH SMITH: You know, you bitch all day nobody in the family takes you seriously and here's your chance to man up and prove you're not the lechero's kid—

WEASEL: It ain't me. It's God. He's got P T S D.

JOSEPH SMITH: Who doesn't?

WEASEL: Julio, what's his trigger?

JOSEPH SMITH: His trigger is blood.

WEASEL: So I go in and we're spraying the place with bullets, kingpins are dying, *there's blood all over the place*, God sees that, it triggers his inner freak-out mechanism, and suddenly he's back in Iraq, they're bombing his ass, killing his friends, his friend's blood's all over him, he's got Mr AK in his hand, looking at me like *my* name's Muhammed Abdullah and *loses* it—and I'm on the receiving end of friendly fire!

JOSEPH SMITH: Yeah, man. Be careful in there.

WEASEL: Am I talking at the ear that don't work?

(WEASEL *goes to* JOSEPH SMITH's *good ear.*)

WEASEL: Yo! Who's home in there?

JOSEPH SMITH: Refrain yourself! God's little melt-down before? That wasn't about Maritza at the airport. It's the whole blood complex. He doesn't want to face the blood.

WEASEL: I JUST SAID AS MUCH AND NO ONE LISTENED.

JOSEPH SMITH: So he's willing to go in there, face the creature that most messes his head, makes him sick to his stomach and turns him inside-out. So what are you and I willing to do?

WEASEL: It ain't about *willing*, it's *denial*—

(GOD *comes in.*)

GOD: Lucy's okay, just having some big-time boriqua freak-out moment. She says if we fuck this up, she's going to grab Janet and Linda and Emily and Madre and they're going to come down here and show us boys how it's done.

JOSEPH SMITH: Whoa! I mean, would you want to get in their way?

GOD: Fuck, no! Where's Buddha's fat ass?

JOSEPH SMITH: Still on the phone to the arms dealer and stuff.

WEASEL: Guys, I'm worried about Buddha's legs. How is he gonna climb those hills up there into position? I mean, look at all the weight he's carrying.

JOSEPH SMITH: You know how many nutrition websites I send him all the time? And basic exercise and yoga?

WEASEL: So what's the problem?

JOSEPH SMITH: Ever since he got laid off, he doesn't take care of himself as much. Like he's giving up. And I tell him, "Man, you know Tommy's watching everything you do. He's learning everything from you. You don't respect yourself and your body, what's Tommy learning with that?"

WEASEL: I could get up those hills and shoot from there. I could *run* up there.

GOD: Really. And Buddha's going to go running in the hideout with me? Key word: *running*?

JOSEPH SMITH: Plus you need two hands to handle an M4 and you can't be holding your dick or a cane.

GOD: And you're real brave when Buddha's back is turned. I want to hear you say this shit to his face.

WEASEL: For real, God. Look at me. Man to man.

GOD: I'm searching around for the other man...

WEASEL: No more bullshit. You can do this? Go in there and shoot people and deal with the blood without going psycho?

GOD: What the fuck you talking about?

WEASEL: You know what. Your thing. Your war thing.

GOD: You need to lay off the fuckin' crack pipe—

WEASEL: You know what I'm talking about—

GOD: You need to lay off the fuckin' crack pipe—

WEASEL: You know what I'm talking about—

GOD: You need to lay off the fuckin' crack pipe—

WEASEL: *You know what I'm talking about—!*

GOD: YOU NEED TO LAY OFF THE FUCKIN' CRACK PIPE—!

(WEASEL grabs GOD. GOD grabs WEASEL. They're face to face. Then GOD smells it.)

GOD: She's fuckin' drunk, isn't she? She's totally wasted!

(He goes to the cooler, drags it to the door—and throws the beer bottles into the street outside.)

(Not feeling well, JOSEPH SMITH clutches his stomach, sits down.)

JOSEPH SMITH: Whoa, someone's talking to me in there…

(GOD throws out the last beer and slams the door shut.)

(The door flies open and BUDDHA enters.)

BUDDHA: Yo, perfectly good beer, motherfucker!

GOD: Shitbird over here is drunk!

JOSEPH SMITH: Guys, I know the last thing we need is a complication…

GOD: Hector, grab some chow and down some water! A direct order!

(WEASEL *doesn't move. He giggles.* GOD *grabs him by the collar and drags him to the food and water.*)

(WEASEL *reluctantly eats crackers and drinks water.*)

BUDDHA: You seen the scenery out there? There are some fuckin' desert queens in this town. In my mind's eye I'm thinking—

GOD: What the gun merchant say?

BUDDHA: —I may have to buy me a little hacienda down here and find me a lil' señorita! Have me a whole brood of Mexo-Ricans!

GOD: You don't shut the fuck up and tell me what's going on, you're going to be buying *funeral land* down here.

BUDDHA: Okay we got us a dealer. Town of Luz de Marta. Perfect name!

GOD: And where the hell is that?

BUDDHA: Middle of bum fuck nowhere, how should I know?

GOD: You don't know how long it takes to get there?

BUDDHA: I ain't from these parts, negro!

GOD: Let's find out, Rain Man, shall we?
(*He goes to his computer.*)

(JOSEPH SMITH *sweats hard, breathes heavy, has to sit down.*)

GOD: Oh look! The computer tells us this town is *an hour and a half* by car.

JOSEPH SMITH: You couldn't find no one closer and stuff?

GOD: The sun sets at 19:15, Dude. How are we going to get all the way out to Kricka de Marta and back by then?

BUDDHA: You wanna get on the horn and talk to them guys? Find someone else?

(GOD *types on the computer.*)

GOD: Alright, fuck it, I've got driving directions, let's do this.

BUDDHA: They call what they talk down here Spanish but, man, I was all kinds of confused with this motherfucker!

(GOD *clocks the agony on* JOSEPH SMITH's *face.*)

GOD: You sure you're cool?

JOSEPH SMITH: Lets do this before everything else goes wrong.

GOD: It's 15:00. Joseph Smith and I will get in the truck and deal with the gun merchant guy. Buddha and Weas' you're on the bikes—

BUDDHA: —Recon the hills for shooting spot half mile from hideout, we know...

GOD: Dude, you're *not* autistic!

BUDDHA: And it's not too late for me to field-strip sections of your face.

GOD: Oh no I just wet myself with fear.

JOSEPH SMITH: Buddha, you're in charge of base camp. Keep his mangina sober if it kills you!

GOD: We get to Kricka de Marta by 16:30. By 17:00, 17:30 at the *latest*, fingers crossed, we're armed like it's Armageddon. No time to test the weapons, just grab and go. Meanwhile Buddha and Weasel are back here from their recon in the hills, crying to Mami, shitting themselves and saying their final prayers. And Weasel you better be completely sober, bitch, or you're in for the ass-whooping of your adult life. 18:30, 19:00, me and Joe Smith are back at base camp ready for the festivities and fireworks and all-out vengeance to begin. 20:00 needs to be our close of business, at the *latest*, people. For you, Weas', that's 8:00 PM. Cuz that's when the cartel begins to dismember our brother *if we don't strike first.*

(GOD *and* JOSEPH SMITH *grab the backpack full of money and leave the room.*)

(There's the sound of a heavy truck starting and pulling quickly away.)

(WEASEL *buries his head in his hands.*)

(BUDDHA *scratches his balls.*)

(Outside, far in the distance, there's the sound of a man screaming. Is it Numb Nuts?)

(BUDDHA *and* WEASEL *listen fearfully.*)

(Black out)

END OF ACT ONE

ACT TWO

(Same day. Same motel. 7:00 PM)

(The suitcases, backpacks and sleeping bags are gone. Most of the food and drink has been consumed.)

(Instead, the room is filled with AK-47s, 9-MM Berettas, Glocks, shoulder holsters, K-bar knives, boxes of ammunition, B Bs, grenades, tanks of propane, gas masks, body armor, and an Airsoft grenade launcher attached to a Colt M4 assault rifle. There are two large empty backpacks.)

(WEASEL is sober and not happy about it. Eating pineapple slices, he and BUDDHA carefully inspect, disassemble, clean, reassemble, and load their weapons, punctuating the dialogue with the metallic snaps and clicks. They load grenades with propane gas and BB's and try on their body armor and gas masks. BUDDHA checks and re-checks the sight on his 7.62 mm Army M24 sniper rifle.)

(The weapons and ammunition have an almost meditative, zen-like influence on BUDDHA and WEASEL. This is something they know how to do. Something they understand. Something that reaffirms a vital but long-buried part of their identities. This is serious fun.)

(GOD paces nervously, lights a cigarette, blows smoke out the door, checks his watch, bites his nails, checks the computer, checks his phone, checks on the arsenal, re-cleans the weapons, etc.)

(JOSEPH SMITH *is in the offstage bathroom. The door to the bathroom is partially open.*)

(*Part way through the act, the sun begins to set, subtly flooding the motel room with red light.*)

GOD: What's your E T A in there, Smith? We've got major time issues in case you don't remember!

JOSEPH SMITH: (*Off*) Whyyyyyyy? Ohhh, whhhhhyyyyyyyyy??

(BUDDHA *is in the middle of a story.*)

BUDDHA: —so we was just chillin' at his place in Brooklyn, like freakin' hipster dudes *everywhere,* and he and Lucy are showing us a real good time, me and Tommy, and I don't even fuckin' know how it got started but suddenly we was on the topic of global warming.

(WEASEL *holds up a Glock.*)

WEASEL: What you pay for this Glock? Calling it a piece of shit is insulting to shit.

(BUDDHA *laughs hard.*)

BUDDHA: He so took the bait! Went from zero to sixty in point-oh seconds, all up in my grill, "Global warming is *real*, Charlie! It's already here! And we did it to ourselves!"

(GOD, *preoccupied, barely listening, continues to pace back and forth.*)

(WEASEL *holds up another Glock.*)

WEASEL: And *this* piece? Are you serious? You guys got ripped, man.

BUDDHA: I told him—totally straight face—there's a reason it's getting warmer and it ain't the people.

(GOD *checks the Glocks.*)

GOD: Dude, please don't tell me we're going to be two sidearms short.

(WEASEL *hands* GOD *the grenade launcher.*)

WEASEL: And serious reservations about this guy!

(*Until he enters later,* JOSEPH SMITH *calls to the others from off.*)

JOSEPH SMITH: If it isn't people's carbon footprint, what did you say it was?

BUDDHA: Told him: the Ice Age is still *ending,* that's why it's warmer outside!

JOSEPH SMITH: I bet that burned his ass!

(GOD *takes apart the grenade launcher.*)

GOD: This baby doesn't work, the whole epic scenario falls to pieces.

WEASEL: It's caked with rust in there. You guys shouldda taken the time to check it.

GOD: There was no motherfucking time, you little dick garage!

JOSEPH SMITH: So what's the weapons status out there?

WEASEL: A shit show!

GOD: We're rolling with a lot of ass today, which we need to use *in less than an hour!*

WEASEL: Those two Glocks are old but usable. But none of this armor's been cleaned in forever. There's old blood stains. And this mask has a hole.

GOD: Was there a reason we didn't buy the weed that knucklehead was trying to sell us?

JOSEPH SMITH: Buddha, you're so deaaaaaad...

BUDDHA: Who told you to eat unwashed grapes in Mexico? You shouldda had the pineapple!

JOSEPH SMITH: I'm gonna take that pineapple and cram it up your culo...oooooooooooo, God make it stoooooooooooop...

WEASEL: At least close the door!

JOSEPH SMITH: It's three hundred degrees if I close the door!

WEASEL: You're killing us!

JOSEPH SMITH: You got gas masks!

GOD: We need you to fuckin' snap to in there! It's designed as a four man operation! We need you or it totally doesn't work!

JOSEPH SMITH: I'm shitting as fast as I can...

BUDDHA: Then we go see this Shakespeare play, I couldn't fuckin' tell you, plot-wise, what was up or down—except this one girl, oh God she was a fine woman—the whole play, all I'm thinking, for three hours, she could get her Titus Andronicus on my bad boy any time!

JOSEPH SMITH: And you couldn't follow the plot? Amazing!

BUDDHA: There was a scene, she takes her shirt off— and I'm turning to Numb Nuts, goin', "Someone hold me back 'cause I'mma jump on stage and devour them puppies!" I think the actress even heard me!

JOSEPH SMITH: You think maybe it's your entire approach to women that's the problem?

BUDDHA: So we're all walking out the theatre and him and me we get into it about the Zombie Apocalypse. Numb Nuts don't even believe in the Zombie Apocalypse!

GOD: Okay, that's where I draw the line.

BUDDHA: He says it's just a random excuse for gun owners to keep their firearms.

JOSEPH SMITH: He's right about that, though...

WEASEL: 'Cause we gotta kill the zombies! Duh!

BUDDHA: I told him how the apocalypse is a government-inspired plot and he almost lost his shit on Houston Street.

GOD: Just ask him, if the government isn't planning a zombie apocalypse then why are they putting out all these zombie movies and T V shows all of a sudden?

JOSEPH SMITH: Uh, why are they putting out all those zombie movies and T V shows all of a sudden?

GOD: To get us fuckin' prepared. It's a warning, Dude, of what's to come.

JOSEPH SMITH: Why would they warn us if they're going to attack us?

GOD: Japan warned us before Pearl Harbor, right? Same thing!

WEASEL: Slam dunk!

JOSEPH SMITH: If your brother were here, he'd be throwing up in his mouth and swallowing.

BUDDHA: So along with the Gulf War, Arabs, hookers, and global warming, I gotta stay away from the topic of the Zombie Apocalypse too.

WEASEL: Pretty soon there ain't nothing to talk about with him.

BUDDHA: Oh, you should see Lucy's face when I say nasty shit about feminists! She's got a temper and she could put a serious hurt on a man!

WEASEL: Someone in their family's gotta be growing actual cojones.

JOSEPH SMITH: Can you grow cojones in Brooklyn?

BUDDHA: I just love fuckin' with their heads with this shit! It's just too easy though!

GOD: Guns are clean! Ammo's set! Put a tampon in it so we can go, Smith!!

JOSEPH SMITH: Almost, almost…

WEASEL: One time, man, he and Lucy were out in Sacramento and we got into politics and he's shitting on me with all his *Harper's Magazine* "progressive" bullshit and he don't respect a word I say, and he's like, "I'm looking around your house, Hec', and you have no books, no magazines or newspapers, where the hell do you get your information if you never *read*? You just regurgitate what talk radio tells you to say?" He called me a "low-information voter!"

BUDDHA: Oh no he didn't.

WEASEL: At my own dinner table! Eating the food I served with my own hands! That I paid for with my hard work!

(GOD *goes to the bathroom door.*)

GOD: Dude, they have a pharmacy in Mexico. I can get you Depends n' shit. You can shit and walk and launch grenades at the same time.

(JOSEPH SMITH *groans.*)

WEASEL: When we were alone, Linda's going, "Your oldest brother just doesn't respect you and that's so sad to me."

BUDDHA: Did you tell her that none of us respect you? Not even Madre? Or my dog?

JOSEPH SMITH: Yeah big brother can be kinda a snob.

WEASEL: A classic prick, you mean.

BUDDHA: So why are we saving his geek ass again?

(GOD *is ready to jump out of his skin, yells at the bathroom.*)

GOD: *ARE YOU GOING TO LIVE? CAN WE DO THIS?*

JOSEPH SMITH: Give me two!

BUDDHA: Big brother don't like guns. He don't like the military. He don't like soldiers. He don't like war.

WEASEL: But guns, the military, and grunts are gonna save his ass today.

JOSEPH SMITH: Cuz he almost went to Vietnam is why.

GOD: *DOES ANYONE BUT ME SEE THE HOLY MOTHER OF GOD TIME?*

JOSEPH SMITH: It kinda haunted him when he was a kid. He turned eighteen, he got his draft notice, and dad wasn't going to let him skip to Canada. But the war ended that same month. It scared him to get so close to that cesspool.

WEASEL: That ain't a war I'd want to be part of.

BUDDHA: When I enlisted, he friggin' took me to a movie to make me change my mind about the Army. *Gallipoli.* We was leaving the theatre and he asks me what I thought of all these scenes of Australian infantry running at the Turkish machine gun nests and getting hammered and he's thinking I'm gonna go, "Oh you're so right, big brother, war is hell! I'm gonna un-enlist right now!" And I said to him, "Well, that was stupid. We don't fight wars that way. No one runs into machine guns any more!" He slapped his forehead so loud you could hear the echo in Kuwait.

WEASEL: All he knows is what he reads in the paper. What the Hollywood geeks tell him.

JOSEPH SMITH: He doesn't understand all the love and goodness that comes with the military. The Meals Rejected by Ethiopia. Murphy in control of every situation. The V A Hospital, the top notch care, all the good drugs.

(Beat as BUDDHA *thinks about this a moment, suddenly very serious…)*

BUDDHA: Nobody don't understands any of that. Especially the fucking, you know—scars and shit.

WEASEL: You feeling sad, Buddha? Need a hug?

JOSEPH SMITH: Someone hug him! He's having feelings!

BUDDHA: Just one feeling and I'm burying it again!

(The guys laugh then turn quiet as BUDDHA *thinks this through.)*

BUDDHA: No, man. No one tells you what the war is gonna mean when you unpack your gear at home. There's all the talk of "heros," but no one gives a real fuck. And then you're supposed to carry on like nothing happened? Pick up with a wife or girlfriend?

WEASEL: I wouldn't want to do this *single.*

BUDDHA: Except there ain't too many women out there willing to give a vet a break if he's got trauma in his veins.

(All the guys, even GOD, *go quiet as they contemplate the truth of this.)*

BUDDHA: If there's something swimming up in you that wants to chew you from the inside-out. And, you know, you could tell your stories 'til you're blue in the face. Take 'em back there so they can fuckin' see the blaze and smell the mayhem. But ain't nothing your words say, ain't no picture you can make in their minds, will ever help them understand.

GOD: Because you don't fucking understand it…

BUDDHA: There's a micro-part of you that's always gonna be beyond reach, beyond all the things a woman has the right to know. And soon you just give up trying to explain your hell.

GOD: And it's all silence.

BUDDHA: Ain't no woman wanna sleep with that silence for too long, I'll tell you from experience.

(A silent agreement and communion among all the brothers for a moment.)

JOSEPH SMITH: Trouble is all the girls you hit on are bartenders in their 20s, bro.

BUDDHA: If it works for Numb Nuts, why can't it work for me?

JOSEPH SMITH: Universe just isn't fair, brother.

(BUDDHA and JOSEPH SMITH share a laugh.)

(GOD, moved by the conversation, is deep in thought.)

GOD: I mean, if Janet wasn't in the Army, I don't know if she would've wanted to marry a soldier. What the fuck for? So she can baby-sit the ghosts? Keep Godzilla out of the bedroom? But she's seen it first hand. She knows about blood and the puke and, like, I don't know—*whatever*, man!

BUDDHA: None of my wives ever got it. Civilians got so fuckin' spoiled, man. They got no fuckin' clue what happens behind their backs, in their name, for their home and safety, that they're *paying* for. Why not be fat, opinionated, and ignint? Like all my exes!

WEASEL: Maybe you could use Madre's brujeria skills to find you a wife, Buddha.

BUDDHA: Naw, she's spending all her chicken mojo trying to get Joseph Smith a husband.

(All the guys laugh. Slap five, bump fists.)

JOSEPH SMITH: You are so lucky my ass is nailed to this toilet, Charlie.

(BUDDHA winks at the others.)

BUDDHA: It's suspicious. You're almost fifty and you ain't never been married. And hardly ever had no girlfriends after the Reagan years. And the one girl who really wanted your ass, who followed you around like a sad puppy, you totally blew her off. There can only be one reason.

JOSEPH SMITH: Maybe it was watching you and Emmy and Weas' and God and Numb Nuts getting divorces and stuff.

GOD: Look, Dude, we're alone. No listening devices. We won't tell Madre. Just tell us you're gay.

JOSEPH SMITH: Maybe I thought, might as well just cut to the chase and stay single and not have the pain, you know?

BUDDHA: You ain't got the patience for a relationship, bro. You gotta eat your breakfast at six am, your lunch at noon, your dinner at six pm or you go postal. God forbid someone puts a cup in the wrong drawer. *Scheisse!* Talk about war!

JOSEPH SMITH: It's my life! Why shouldn't I have it the way I want it and stuff? I fight in the military. I lose buddies in a helicopter crash in the desert. I get a discharge. I'm homeless until the Mormons help me. Now? I'm employed. I run a whole engineering department at Sanmina. So haven't I earned the right to live like I want?

BUDDHA: If it means you don't got a woman and you're still a virgin, maybe!

JOSEPH SMITH: *I am not a virgin! Bone*-head! And don't you think I get lonely too? Don't you think I'd like to be with somebody? Share laughs and stuff? Even be a dad?

(Getting caught up in the camaraderie, even GOD starts losing track of time.)

GOD: Joe Smith, you'd be a totally great dad. But the first step is you need a female sperm receptacle.

WEASEL: And Siri don't count!

JOSEPH SMITH: But she's hot!

BUDDHA: Can't you see Joseph Smith teaching his son sex education? "Son, I *think*. But I'm not *sure*. I only seen one once in my life, and even then I had my eyes closed and I was scared and confused. But I think *that's* a vagina. I ain't too sure what you do with it, though."

JOSEPH SMITH: Buddha, I have something to say to you...

BUDDHA: "Son, there's this thing called 'giving head' but I honestly can't tell you what that means."

GOD: Oh, Chucky, you just don't know when to stop...

JOSEPH SMITH: But, you know, sometimes I'm not totally in sync with the way you're raising Tommy right now.

BUDDHA: Aw, fuckin' here we go with this shit...

JOSEPH SMITH: I see you guys every day. And I'm not the only one who thinks this neither.

BUDDHA: Do I look like I give a single good fuck what people think about me and my son?

JOSEPH SMITH: He's always on your lap. You're always holding him, giving him kisses. And when he cries, you always pick him up. Buttoning his coat, tying his shoes, wiping his nose...

BUDDHA: Now you're saying I can't love my son? Let me help you grasp the obvious here—

JOSEPH SMITH: I'm not talking about love! But he's getting too old for that shit. He's nine, time to cut the umbilical chord, brother, or he's never going to grow up and learn to be a man.

BUDDHA: Being a man ain't the only thing I need to teach him—

JOSEPH SMITH: But it's the most important thing. How to respect himself. How to size up an adversary. How to think for himself. How to take apart a broken machine and get it to work. How to *survive*. He's not going to survive by crying to daddy every five minutes. He's going to be dependent and weak. Maybe 'cause Dad never gave you what you needed, it's no reason to get carried away and smother your son.

(His formidable temper kicking in, Buddha goes to the bathroom door and yells.)

BUDDHA: Well you ain't never HAD a son—and you ain't never WILL have a son—SO SHUT THE FUCK UP!

JOSEPH SMITH: Look, you don't want to cross a line with me!

BUDDHA: Or what? You gonna hit me with your *purse*? You're nothing but an *old woman*. You live this unreal life, man, with no relationships, nothing connecting you to nobody, no one touching you or getting near you, no one to need you or give you nothing—so you leave no mark on the fuckin' world. You leave no trace. Like you're an *idea* of a man that God never got around to actually *make*. I swear, man, you're so fuckin' afraid of life you're gonna be dead before you fuckin' even live it!

(BUDDHA kicks a hole in the wall.)

(A long silence as everyone takes this outburst in and no one looks at each other.)

(The offstage sound of a toilet flushing.)

(JOSEPH SMITH, pale, ill, and unsteady, walks weakly into the room, clutching his stomach and the wall. The guys look at him, amused and worried.)

JOSEPH SMITH: I suggest no one go in there for the next ten weeks. And stuff.

GOD: Okay! We need to mobilize *on the double*. Okay, lets step-by-step the operation one more time...

*(*JOSEPH SMITH'*s phone rings. "Come Sail Away." He looks at the incoming number. The others all look at him warily. With a bone-deep weary sigh, he answers.)*

JOSEPH SMITH: Yes, Ma. Si. Si. Lucy told you? Shit!

(The brothers react silently to the news that their mother knows about their mission.)

*(*JOSEPH SMITH *listens for a long moment. Puts on his solicitous voice.)*

JOSEPH SMITH: Why did I lie to you about the otters? Well, I had to. Because I knew you would cry. Am I right? Did you cry? Ma, he's going to be alright. We have this under control. Yes, all of us are here. In Mexico.

(Waits while his mother wails)

Ma! Nothing's going to happen to your precious oldest son, Ma. All of us are going to be very careful and we know what we're doing and we trained for this—sure, it was a long time ago, but still—and we're going to hurt a lot of bad guys who take a lot of drugs and don't believe in the Holy Ghost, Ma, and we're going to bring Numb—bring your precious hijo major pendejo stupido feo back home with us. And you can go back to pretending he's your favorite when you know that I am.

WEASEL: I am!

BUDDHA: I am!

GOD: I'm in kindergarten.

JOSEPH SMITH: Can you trust me on this? Can you take off the Grumpy Face? And I don't know why you're on

the phone when you know this is your nap time. And
I got you those wicked new blankets so you won't be
cold. And the T V is set to your telenovela if you can't
sleep. Okay? Put Tommy on. Tommy. I don't have time
to talk. Do whatever you can to keep her from a total
apocalypse, okay? Okay, bye.
(To the others)
She's all jacked up 'cause she thinks she's going lose all
of us.

*(Hearing about their mother's distress effects all the men
deeply and silences them a moment.)*

WEASEL: What now? Abort?

(GOD looks at his watch.)

GOD: Fuck it, dude, just drive on.

JOSEPH SMITH: I second that.
(He suddenly leans against the wall.)

BUDDHA: Uh, you okay there, big brother?

(JOSEPH SMITH's too angry at BUDDHA to look at him.)

JOSEPH SMITH: Where my nukes at?

GOD: Glock. Rounds. Body armor. And the Airsoft.

BUDDHA: I loaded B Bs and propane into your
cartridges, Julio, they're ready to rock and roll.

(JOSEPH SMITH ignores BUDDHA.)

GOD: You know your face is a kind of zucchini shade of
green, don't you?

JOSEPH SMITH: I'm good to go. Once a Marine, always a
Marine, right, Hec'?

(WEASEL gives JOSEPH SMITH a reluctant smile.)

WEASEL: Semper fi, my brother.

(JOSEPH SMITH and WEASEL bump fists.)

GOD: You two want to do a little oorah circle jerk, I'll turn my head and wait.

JOSEPH SMITH: Hand me that donut launcher.

(GOD hands JOSEPH SMITH the grenade launcher and demonstrates how it works.)

GOD: Totally Marine proof. Press here. Stick the ordnance up this hole—you can *pretend* it's sex—then close her up. Safety on, safety off. I know the Airsoft and she's got some distance on her. Just keep shooting until you hit something that goes ba-da-boom.

BUDDHA: *Big* ba-da-boom!

WEASEL: Multi-pass!

JOSEPH SMITH: You see how rusted out this is? It's going to work?

GOD: It just HAS TO or I will SULK.

JOSEPH SMITH: Let's saddle up.

GOD: First you and Chucklehead need to be okay. *Total* okay. Because I'm not going out there and risk my neck with a divided army. Dissent and bad feelings are the quickest way to get us killed.

(BUDDHA and JOSEPH SMITH regard each other a long, tense moment.)

BUDDHA: I'm totally fuckin' good, ask him.

JOSEPH SMITH: It's all good in the hood, brother.

GOD: Then kiss on the lips and make up.

JOSEPH SMITH: I'd rather shit my brains out.

BUDDHA: See? He got no respect for me, no matter what I do, and I got no fuckin' idea why! Do you know how hard I work for him to say, "Hey, that's cool, Charlie." "Hey, I like the way you handled that, Charlie." "Hey, I can learn from that, Charlie."

(JOSEPH SMITH *breaks out into a grin.*)

JOSEPH SMITH: Shut up, Buddha, and get your dopey, melodramatic, pity-party ass over here...

(BUDDHA *goes to* JOSEPH SMITH *and they embrace. They kiss each other.*)

BUDDHA: I know you seen a vagina once. It wasn't *human*, but at least you saw it...

JOSEPH SMITH: You're right, it was yours.

BUDDHA: That's supposed to be our little secret!

GOD: However dysfunctional, we have ourselves a combat unit! Lock and load, troops! It's time to collect our shit, move out, and hurt bad people!

JOSEPH SMITH: —No. Oh no. Oh no!
(*He suddenly rushes back into the bathroom.*)

GOD: Twenty past seven! That's T-minus forty minutes, dude—and counting!

(*Until he enters later,* JOSEPH SMITH *calls to the others from off.*)

JOSEPH SMITH: Okay, okay, I'm almost. Ooooh, I think I just dropped my pancreas. Yep, that's a pancreas...

GOD: If this continues then we need a work-around.

JOSEPH SMITH: No, I'm good...

GOD: You been at it forty-five minutes! You got an endless supply of shit! There's crap coming out of you from mofongo you ate in 1986!

WEASEL: I know you think you're the actual God, God, but you're not facing the truth, man. Is he gonna be able to even fire that thing? Even if he got off the head in time?

GOD: All he has to do is stand in position, aim, squeeze the trigger, and hop his tubby ass on the bike.

BUDDHA: Can you handle that much, Julio?

(JOSEPH SMITH *groans*.)

WEASEL: Motherfucker can't even stand or see or breathe—

GOD: Fine! I can fire the Airsoft. Smith can drive the get-away truck.

WEASEL: You're gonna fire a grenade launcher in broad daylight, from a park across the street, then sprint your old ass two hundred yards to the hideout, and *no one seeing you*?

GOD: I've done harder and worse in the field when you were a fuckin' desk rat hiding behind a typewriter.

BUDDHA: Every eye is gonna be on the mushroom cloud, Hec'—that makes God invisible.

WEASEL: Running around with body armor, a gas mask around his face, and an AK-47? That's not conspicuous?

GOD: Yeah, yeah, just shut up and color…

WEASEL: I'm so tired being the one calling your endless bullshit and no one fucking listens.

GOD: Who heard a noise? There a fly in the room?

WEASEL: I love my brother, even if he makes me postal, even when he's calling me Neanderthal to my face, a fucking gun-nut who don't read. Even if he shits on everything I value and it's bad men like me corrupting this world. I would do anything for him but I won't die for him. And you know what's up with that? He wouldn't ask me to. Because he wouldn't risk breaking the lives of Linda and Stevie and Mom.

GOD: So we don't answer this insult to our family? To our fuckin' country? Is that what we teach them fuckers?

BUDDHA: Buy a couple of Aztec souvenirs at the airport and go home?

WEASEL: We march into their hideout. Man to man. And we negotiate a settlement…

GOD: And say pretty please? Bend over like we like it?

BUDDHA: Then they take us? So now they got five of us? Madre will love that!

JOSEPH SMITH: We don't negotiate with terrorists!

WEASEL: We rushed into this. Like blind. Like we got all macho on ourselves. We didn't think. We didn't try everything else first.

GOD: When was there time?

WEASEL: Numb Nuts got friends who are Spooks and politicians and movie stars and millionaires and shit. They can't put pressure on these guys? Don't he know somebody, who knows somebody, who knows somebody? Ain't there a whole film studio who needs his ass?

GOD: Dude, he's a writer.

JOSEPH SMITH: Straight to D V D!

WEASEL: But don't he got like a million people on Twitter or some shit? Can't they do something to mobilize the press?

GOD: We didn't try Face Book! What is wrong with us? Please like my page— "Saving Private Numb Nuts!"

WEASEL: A couple of hours ago you wanted to go home. But the more time you spend down here, acting all G I Joe, the Nazier you get.

GOD: And why can't you just deal? Why are you bellyaching this whole time since Sacramento? I think there's a simple answer.

WEASEL: I ain't getting into a big dick contest with you…

GOD: You have a valor deficit. You have issues with courage. You possess a high chicken shit quotient.

WEASEL: I don't wanna be no bullet-stopper? Yes! Dying scares me? Shit, I must be outta my mind that I'm scared of fighting an organized gang of young, crazy, armed, vicious, narco drug traffickers in their own backyard!

GOD: It ain't about scared. We're all scared.

BUDDHA: I am basically shitless over here.

JOSEPH SMITH: A grunt who isn't scared isn't human.

GOD: You think I want to face the blood? And Buddha wants to feel exposed to danger like he did stepping out of that tank into the desert in Iraq? Brave, scared— who gives a fuck? It's how you *respond* to fear. It's about the *honesty* of that response. You? You don't stop motherfucking *pretending*, Dude. That's what pisses me off. It's like when you got your tattoo in high school…

WEASEL: We're really going to go back to *high* school?

GOD: Your little winged unicorn tattoo. Little Pegasus with a horn. Which you covered up after we gave you so much shit. Buried it under the face of Satan!

WEASEL: That's your beef? Get a fucking life!

GOD: If you fuckin' wanna wear a little pink My Favorite Pony tattoo, then have the honesty and the balls to wear it!

JOSEPH SMITH: Not pink! Lavender!

GOD: It's like that fuckin' story you tell. How you were all set to go to Desert Storm.

WEASEL: If Joseph Smith don't come out of the head in two minutes, I'm packing up and this mission is done.

GOD: Bragging how you were all ready to go in-country and man up, and they pulled you off the plane at the last minute because Congress discovered you already had two brothers in the war.

WEASEL: I can show you the papers.

GOD: That never happened, Hector. It never happened. You spent the first Persian Gulf War knocking on doors at high schools getting ghetto kids to enlist because you speak Spanish.

BUDDHA: A combat soldier never brags about being a war hero…

WEASEL: I tell it 'cause it's fucking true!

GOD: You tell it because you're forty-three and you're still pretending. Because you're the only non-combat vet in this room. And that fuckin' embarrasses you. But you know what? Fuck that shit. You think we don't love you because you didn't go to Iraq with us? You don't fuckin' get it through your skull that not every soldier needs to be in the field. What you were fuckin' doing out there, going door to door in Oakland and South Central and whatever, that's part of the war too. That's fuckin' *valuable*. You show up in your dress blues, looking mean and proud, that's valuable to the armed forces. It's a contribution to your nation's defense.

BUDDHA: That's the shit right there.

GOD: If you stopped hiding behind "oh I'm the baby of the family" shit. "Oh, all of you abandoned me one by one" shit. "Oh, you left me alone with Dad and he never took me to the pony rides" shit!

BUDDHA: That man took none of us to the pony rides.

GOD: You fuckin' think it's all about guns. But it isn't about the size of your arsenal. Firing a weapon won't make a man out of you and plenty of good men went to their deaths without ever firing a shot.

BUDDHA: Now you're fuckin' scaring me 'cause now you're channeling Numb Nuts and Oprah...

(The toilet flushes.)

(JOSEPH SMITH enters. He looks worse. Takes one step into the room, unsteady, like he can't see—opens his mouth— nothing comes out, but—)

JOSEPH SMITH: Uhhhhhhhhhhhhhhhhhh...
(And he falls flat on his face.)

GOD: Man down!

(The brothers rush to JOSEPH SMITH and turn him over.)

WEASEL: Loosen his belt, let him breathe.

(BUDDHA loosens JOSEPH SMITH's belt.)

BUDDHA: Julio, can you hear us?

GOD: Can you sit up? Julio?

BUDDHA: Brother, can you hear us?

GOD: Talk to me! Turn away from the light!

WEASEL: Insult the Mormon Church, maybe that'll get his attention.

(JOSEPH SMITH's breathing is ragged. GOD clears some space on one of the beds, pushing the Glocks aside.)

BUDDHA: Let's get him on the bed. On three. One, two—

(With much effort, the brothers lift JOSEPH SMITH, nearly drop him on the floor, but manage to lay him on the bed.)

(WEASEL runs to the bathroom as BUDDHA fans JOSEPH SMITH.)

(GOD goes to the groceries and pulls out a bottle of Mountain Dew.)

(WEASEL *returns with a damp towel which he places over* JOSEPH SMITH*'s forehead.)*

(GOD *and* BUDDHA *help* JOSEPH SMITH *sit up.* GOD *puts the bottle of Mountain Dew to his lips and* JOSEPH SMITH *slowly sips it.)*

(*As* JOSEPH SMITH *sips Mountain Dew, some color seems to return to his face and light into his eyes.)*

(*The brothers look at him, relieved.* JOSEPH SMITH *smiles weakly.)*

GOD: Okay. I got a Plan B work-around designed for a three-man team and it's pretty simple, even you can understand it, Buddha.

JOSEPH SMITH: …No, Tony.

BUDDHA: He fuckin' speaks! Welcome to the world!

GOD: What do you mean "no?"

JOSEPH SMITH: There's no three-man scenario that can work. It's a guaranteed suicide with three. We have to abort.

WEASEL: Finally, I'm not the only one with some commonsense in the goddamn room!

GOD: You look in my eyes and tell me this? Now that we're *this close*?

(JOSEPH SMITH *wheezes as he speaks.)*

JOSEPH SMITH: Numb Nuts was my first friend. When I had the motorcycle accident, he came to stay with me. He cooked. It sucked, but he cooked. He helped me out when I was lost after my discharge and I was living on the beach, eating kelp. But.
(Beat)
But I'm not going to lose all my brothers on the same day, I'm just not…

(JOSEPH SMITH *has to fight to keep from getting tearful. The brothers take in the rare sight in silence. Until...*)

GOD: Fuck, he's having feelings...

(JOSEPH SMITH *lies back down and closes his eyes, exhausted.*)

(BUDDHA, GOD, *and* WEASEL *look at each other.*)

(WEASEL *starts packing up.*)

GOD: Buddha!

(BUDDHA *and* GOD *walk to the far side of the room and whisper.*)

BUDDHA: Talk to me.

GOD: You down for three?

BUDDHA: I'm down for fucking *one*.

GOD: Abort the sniper.

BUDDHA: Radical!

GOD: You fire the Airsoft, create the diversion.

BUDDHA: And I can grab the M4, provide cover.

GOD: I go in solo for the extraction.

BUDDHA: Weasel drives the get-away truck.

GOD: It's a war plan.

BUDDHA: It's done, motherfucker.

(JOSEPH SMITH *weakly sits up.*)

JOSEPH SMITH: I heard that.

BUDDHA: Oh no, it lives!

JOSEPH SMITH: And I'll swear to you on la kricka de Marta that it's not going to happen without the full four-man force.

GOD: Enjoy the ringside seat, Smith, 'cause this is going down.

JOSEPH SMITH: Why? So Madre can lose four sons, Emmy and I lose four brothers, Lucy loses a husband and three brothers-in-law, Janet loses a husband and three brothers-in-law, Linda loses a husband and three brothers-in-law, Stevie loses a father and three uncles, Tommy loses a—

BUDDHA: OKAY STOP RIGHT THERE.

JOSEPH SMITH: These are the lives you're playing with, Tony.

GOD: You know how many missions I ran in Iraq? All by myself? Dropping in behind enemy lines? Just me and a radio and a couple of prayers? Just me with my hand over my balls cause I was so scared? Just me imagining myself a P O W—and them fanatics *beheading* me? You know how many times I *survived* that? This baby-wipe operation is *nothing*. There are ten dick-heads out there standing between me and my brother—and I can take them with my eyes fucking closed! Okay? I will succeed at this, like I succeed at everything—

WEASEL: One of us is going to die—

GOD: *—and there will be zero Iglesia casualties on this day!*

(JOSEPH SMITH picks up one of the Glocks and aims it at GOD.)

(A long moment of stillness and silence)

JOSEPH SMITH: I can stop you.

GOD: My eyes are playing a fucking mirage on me!

(WEASEL's weak laugh.)

WEASEL: It is a mirage 'cause that's the goddamn Glock that don't work.

JOSEPH SMITH: What? Cabrón!

(JOSEPH SMITH *throws the Glock. It hits a lamp and shatters it.*)

BUDDHA: Orale, carnal! Chingao, esse!

(The brothers look at each other in silence—and then start laughing.)

(It starts out small, with one brother, and grows, engulfing all of them in a primal, chaotic, big belly laughter and coughing and stomping that shakes the motel room.)

(It goes on for a while and no one notices JOSEPH SMITH's *phone ringing—"Come Sail Away" plays—until it's almost too late.)*

(JOSEPH SMITH *looks at the incoming number.*)

GOD: Don't answer it!

(JOSEPH SMITH *weakly answers it.*)

JOSEPH SMITH: Lucy, what's—? Lucy—I can't understand. Lucy—the *what*? Video? There's a video?

*(*GOD *goes to his computer and pulls up his email.)*

BUDDHA: They send another one?

WEASEL: We got like an half hour left—

GOD: You expect those criminal, lying motherfuckers to play by their own rules and listen to deadlines? God, we've been so fuckin' stupid!
(He downloads the video and watches it in silence.)

(JOSEPH SMITH *continues on the phone with Lucy.*)

JOSEPH SMITH: Lu'—. Lu'—. Lucy—uh-huh—*what?*...
(He listens a long moment, incredulous.)
...Lucy? Hello? She hung up. She buying tickets to Mexico. She's bringing Janet, Emily, and Linda with her. What the hell's going on?

GOD: They cut his hand off.

(Silence. No one can move.)

(Then on JOSEPH SMITH'*s signal,* BUDDHA *and* WEASEL *help* JOSEPH SMITH *to his feet. It takes all their strength and* JOSEPH SMITH *is extremely unsteady, but they manage to walk him to the computer. The brothers watch the gruesome video in silence.)*

(Everything in the room seems to slow down…)

WEASEL: That ain't him.

GOD: Dude, I don't know…

BUDDHA: They're fucking with our heads—

JOSEPH SMITH: Isn't that his wedding ring?

BUDDHA: They couldda taken it from him. Put it on someone else's hand.

GOD: I think that could be him…

JOSEPH SMITH: …Alright.

BUDDHA: Is that fuckin' him or not?

JOSEPH SMITH: Alright.

GOD: THIS ISN'T FUCKIN' MOTHERFUCKERING RIGHT! I NEED TO SEND SOME PEOPLE TO HEAVEN RIGHT NOW!

JOSEPH SMITH: Alright, alright, alright, alright— *ALRIIIIIIGHT!!* I'm back, people!

GOD: Don't be fucking with me—

JOSEPH SMITH: I'm saying grunts have their orders and we have no time. We need to go, troops. All four of us.

GOD: Right, Weas'? We need to go.

*(*WEASEL *stares at the image on the screen a long moment.)*

WEASEL: All four of us.

GOD: You know the worst part of this? Without his right hand, that's half his sex life gone.

(The others do their best not to laugh but can't help it.)

JOSEPH SMITH: That's cold, even for you, Tony.

GOD: Okay! Joseph Smith, congrats, Plan C dictates
you are driving the get-away vehicle. Buddha, you're
back to sniping, I've got the pea-shooter, I'm going to
hit the depot, and then Weasel and I are going to storm
the hideout.

JOSEPH SMITH: I've got this, Ton'. I can do the grenade
launcher.

GOD: Are you sure? Because you look—

JOSEPH SMITH: The depot's got my name on it. So stop
wasting my time and lets get Buddha ready to deploy.

BUDDHA: Yes! Let's light this fuckin' candle!

(GOD *and* JOSEPH SMITH *help* BUDDHA *on with his body
armor. It barely contains him.* BUDDHA *covers the armor
with a Hawaiian shirt. He looks wildly ridiculous.*)

(WEASEL *puts the sections of* BUDDHA's *disassembled
sniper rifle into one of the backpacks. He fills the pack with
boxes of rounds.*)

(BUDDHA *checks his sidearm and ammunition.*)

(*Suddenly,* GOD *seems to be the most nervous of all the
brothers.*)

(BUDDHA *is holstered up and ready to go. A moment of
silence as everyone takes this in.*)

(GOD *"inspects"* BUDDHA.)

GOD: Yo. Siddhartha. What are your orders?

BUDDHA: Ride into pre-selected position on the bike.
Assemble and position the M24 behind cover of rocks.

GOD: The sun's going to be *exactly* in their eyes. I
planned it perfectly! I am Wiley Coyote—*genius!*

BUDDHA: Back to reality. Get the two vatos on the roof
in my sights. Then wait for the depot explosion. Pick
off the look-outs first. Then the perimeter. Then the

narcos running to the burning gas dump. Cover fire for Joseph Smith as he makes his get-away and the extraction begins, proceeds, and ends.

GOD: Like I said, you're not autistic.

BUDDHA: Imma hang you from my gun turret.

GOD: I love you too. Stay frosty out there.

(GOD and BUDDHA embrace and kiss. BUDDHA goes to JOSEPH SMITH.)

JOSEPH SMITH: You look beat to death.

BUDDHA: Just suckin' on wind at this point.

JOSEPH SMITH: You're my hero, homey.

BUDDHA: Get those cataracts worked on, you dumb fuck.

JOSEPH SMITH: Watch those knees and that chest, shit-for-brains.

BUDDHA: You don't even wanna know what pain I'm in. Why didn't nobody get aspirin?

(JOSEPH SMITH laughs.)

JOSEPH SMITH: Lets get them knees wrapped before you hike.

(BUDDHA pulls his pants down. JOSEPH SMITH carefully unwraps BUDDHA's knees and re-wraps them—a ritual they've shared together before.)

BUDDHA: Weird, you know, in Desert Storm I was in a tank. And you look at these little monitors and the enemy is just a dot and then there's a green flare on the screen and that's how you know you made your kill. Don't know what it's like to kill a man with a face, you know?

(JOSEPH SMITH finishes wrapping BUDDHA's knees. BUDDHA and JOSEPH SMITH embrace and kiss.)

JOSEPH SMITH: Keep your head down. I love you.

BUDDHA: I love you too.

(BUDDHA *goes to* WEASEL.)

WEASEL: In twenty-four hours we're gonna be drinking margaritas back home and laughing about this, right?

BUDDHA: In twenty-four hours I'm gonna be hugging my son Tommy like it's the end of the world.

(BUDDHA *and* WEASEL *embrace and kiss.*)

WEASEL: Love you.

BUDDHA: Love you.

(BUDDHA *grabs his cane and heavy backpack, looks at his brothers. They have no idea what condition they'll find themselves in when they see each other again—or if they'll see each other ever again.*)

(*Nobody wants* BUDDHA *to go yet—*BUDDHA *least of all.* GOD *can see the anxiety and uncertainty in* BUDDHA'*s eyes and face. His body shakes almost imperceptibly.*)

GOD: Chuckles, I think you were in sixth grade. They took you to MacArthur Airport on a field trip and they had a main battle tank from Vietnam there…

BUDDHA: M48 Patton.

GOD: And they let you rug rats climb all over it and inside it and play with all the dials and swing like baboons off the gun turret. And you had the fuckin' time of your life. And that's when you decided to be a soldier.

BUDDHA: I didn't know you remembered that.

GOD: I didn't. Numb Nuts told me that story.

(BUDDHA *turns to leave the room. His backpack knocks into the television, it falls to the ground and breaks.* GOD, JOSEPH SMITH, *and* WEASEL *laugh.*)

BUDDHA: I almost got out of here without breakin' shit!

GOD: Fuckin' Rain Man! You're a waste of good air! Go already!

(Every glass surface in the room has been broken—every window, mirror, lamp, now the T V. Laughing, BUDDHA is out the door.)

(In a moment, there's the sound of a motorcycle trying to start. But it's not working. The brothers go to the window.)

JOSEPH SMITH: I told that lazy moron to check the bike and he said he did and he didn't!

(The motorcycle continues to have trouble starting.)

GOD: FUCK, IS THAT A COP?! Buddha! Get back here!

(There's the roar of the motorcycle—loud, like it's in the room with them…then the roar getting further away…until it's completely silent.)

(BUDDHA's absence is enormous. It takes the remaining brothers some moments to get adjusted to it and not show how much this absence effects them.)

(GOD looks at his watch.)

GOD: It's going to be a few minutes before he's at location.

JOSEPH SMITH: Let's get me suited up.

(GOD and WEASEL help JOSEPH SMITH on with his body armor. JOSEPH SMITH covers the armor with a shirt. It looks strange and bulky.)

(JOSEPH SMITH loads the grenade launcher and grenades into a back pack. He puts on his holster and checks and rechecks his sidearm.)

(GOD looks nervously at his phone.)

(We wait a solid minute in silence.)

GOD: ...be there, be there, be there, be there, be there, be there, be there, be there, be there, be there, be there...

JOSEPH SMITH: *God, can you please?!*

(More silence—more waiting—then GOD *gets the text.)*

GOD: Yes! *The eagle has landed, motherfucker...!*

JOSEPH SMITH: Oh, thank God.

WEASEL: Yeah okay...

GOD: Alright good, whew, it's going to take him a few minutes to climb his fat ass from the road and into firing position.

*(*GOD *stares at his phone. Everyone waits. Another minute in silence.)*

WEASEL: God, let his knees hold up...

GOD: When's he going to get that operation? He's like been in the crutch brigade for like a year.

JOSEPH SMITH: VA won't operate until he loses the weight first. His pain threshold must be insane.

GOD: I can only stand his goofiness so long, and I give him so much shit, but, damn...

JOSEPH SMITH: Even with a bum leg, I've seen him take apart these two puke rednecks half his age at a biker bar, and trust me, it wasn't pretty. And he's loyal like you can't believe.

WEASEL: Come on, Chucky, you can make it up there...

(In the tense silence, GOD *and* WEASEL *get on their body armor. They check their holsters, sidearms, AK-47s and ammunition. They check their smoke, concussion, and frag grenades.)*

*(*GOD *gets the text.)*

GOD: Shooter's in the sniper's nest!

(JOSEPH SMITH and WEASEL embrace joyfully.)

(Silence. GOD gets the next text.)

GOD: We are unpacked.

(Silence. Text)

GOD: We are assembled.

(Silence. Text)

GOD: We're in position.

(Silence. Text)

GOD: We've got the hideout in our sights. Yo, Joseph Smith!

JOSEPH SMITH: Reporting for duty.

GOD: You forgot the "sir".

JOSEPH SMITH: You forgot to suck my dick. Sir. And I'll tell you this now, I really hated calling you God.

GOD: What are you orders, Private?

JOSEPH SMITH: Locate myself behind the latrines in the park. Fire repeatedly at the gas and oil depot until it goes up in flames. Then hightail my ass out of there. Ditch the Virago and deliver the truck to the hideout door to receive the package.

GOD: You forgot the "sir", again.

(JOSEPH SMITH laughs, adjusts his holster, armor. Speaks to them both, but the speech is really for WEASEL—)

JOSEPH SMITH: I know it's stupid to tell you to be careful once you guys are in there. But be mindful. Don't lose your heads. If this works the way I think it will, all the narcos will be gone by the time you break in. Once inside, you've got one duty and that's to extract our brother and to bring him to safety. The mission cannot creep into something bigger, something we can't handle. Okay? No saving the world today.

GOD: If there are fuckin' kids in there, I'm going to get them out, Dude, all of them, so fuck it.

WEASEL: Me too. Pablo and Rosita, man.

GOD: Pablo and Rosita!

JOSEPH SMITH: Okay, whatever. Oorah!

WEASEL: OORAH!

GOD: Uhm. *Oo-rah...?*

JOSEPH SMITH: Wow, with a little more testosterone you could actually pass for a Marine.

GOD: Oh hold on, I think I feel myself giving a fuck, I think I feel it, nope, didn't happen.

(GOD and JOSEPH SMITH embrace and kiss.)

(JOSEPH SMITH looks at WEASEL.)

JOSEPH SMITH: I know you're not used to this. But God is the best there is. He's done this a million times and has all the stupid chest candy to prove it. Just follow his orders and his lead, and you're okay, okay?

WEASEL: I got this.

(JOSEPH SMITH and WEASEL embrace and kiss.)

JOSEPH SMITH: Tell Buddha to get ready to fire. Joseph Smith is wobbling into position.

GOD: Copy that.

(JOSEPH SMITH looks at the grenade launcher dubiously.)

JOSEPH SMITH: And praying this piece of shit works.
(He looks at his brothers one last time then steps outside.)

(Another huge presence is gone and GOD and WEASEL feel the absence acutely. They try very hard not to get emotional, stressed.)

(GOD texts BUDDHA.)

GOD: "Yo, Buddha. Joseph Smith. Is outside the wire. Stand by for orders."

(WEASEL *fidgets nervously with his gear. Drinks Mountain Dew. Checks his sidearm. His ammunition*)

(GOD *watches him.*)

WEASEL: I got through Parris Island. This should be a piece of cake, right, God?

GOD: Are you talking to me, or are you talking to the other God?

WEASEL: Both maybe.

GOD: Here's what my little crystal ball tells me, Hec'.

WEASEL: Crap. Hit me.

GOD: When the depot goes big ba-da-boom—

WEASEL: Multi-pass!

GOD: —and Buddha annihilates the look-outs, I'm making straight for the hideout in the ensuing chaos. But you, your orders are changed. You're staying here, crouched at the open doorway, use the chest of drawers for cover, and from there you're going to provide some fire.

WEASEL: Wait, *what*—?

GOD: I've had plenty of experience in Iraq and Bosnia going it alone.

WEASEL: This can't be done alone.

GOD: If anyone can do it, I can do it.

WEASEL: Who's gonna have your back?

GOD: They call me God for a reason—

WEASEL: I'm going in with you. This ain't even open for discussion—

GOD: I don't need a baby sitter…

WEASEL: *I'm not a fuckin' baby sitter, I'm a fuckin' Marine!*

(Beat)

And I will have your back, 'cause you might think
you're God, but I know what happens. I've always
known what blood does to you. And I knew it, not
'cause you ever told me about it, but 'cause our
brothers told me. 'Cause you would never tell me
something like that for some reason I can't, and will
never, understand. For some reason Weasel is not
included in the family news as far as you're concerned.
But blood causes you to hyperventilate, it chokes your
breathing, you start seeing double, you vomit, and you
are prone to passing out. If you don't pass out, you fall
to your knees and cry uncontrollably. You become a
child. If that happens in there and you're alone and no
one has your back, this entire farce of a rescue is done.
Numb Nuts is done. You need a fellow soldier who
happens to be in the best shape in this family— 'cause
I run half-marathons, yo! —whose knees are actually
good, who don't got cataracts or gout or nightmares
and ain't deaf! You need a fellow soldier to keep
you alert, focused, on task and alive long enough to
carry out your duties. Not you, not nobody, not even
Congress, is gonna pull me out of this combat mission.
Is that clear? Sir?

(Beat)

GOD: You actually finish those half-marathons?

WEASEL: You should run one with me. If your baggy
old mangina can handle the stress.

(GOD and WEASEL embrace and kiss.)

GOD: Glad it's you in there with me.

*(GOD and WEASEL put on their packs. Their gas masks.
They shoulder their AK-47s. They punch each other, blowing
off nervous energy.)*

(GOD *gets the text.*)

GOD: Joseph Smith is in position.

WEASEL: Tell him it's time to get it on.

(GOD *is at the point of no return. The magnitude of the moment hits him. He hesitates, looks at his phone.*)

WEASEL: —Ton'? 'Sup?

(GOD *snaps out of his reverie and texts.*)

GOD: "Buddha. Stand. By. Smith. Stand. By."

WEASEL: What?

(GOD *looks at* WEASEL, *thinking, making his decision with a deep breath.*)

GOD: You know what really happened at the airport today? Janet told me why she's been getting sick every morning. So it looks like we're going for number two. Ain't that a kick in the head?

WEASEL: Really happy for you.

(*Hands trembling,* GOD *texts.*)

GOD: "Joseph Smith. Time to light 'em up. And bring the package home."

(GOD *and* WEASEL *go to the windows and wait in silence.*)

(*A massive explosion rocks the motel room. Blinding flashes of light blast them from every direction.*)

(GOD *and* WEASEL, *the light of the fire reflecting on their bodies, watch the growing mushroom cloud in silence.*)

(*We hear angry men shout in Spanish.*)

(*We hear* JOSEPH SMITH's *motorcycle take off at full speed— the sound disappears in the distance.*)

(*We hear bullets—as* BUDDHA *shoots—and men scream and fall. It's chaos and mayhem.*)

(GOD *watches the situation outside and likes what he sees. He nods to* WEASEL.)

(WEASEL *nods back: good to go.*)

(GOD *and* WEASEL *charge through the door and disappear in the bright red desert sunset.*)

(*The sound of escalating machine gun fire, screams, explosions.*)

(*Dead silence and black out*)

END OF PLAY

www.ingramcontent.com/pod-product-compliance
Lightning Source LLC
Chambersburg PA
CBHW052207090426
42741CB00010B/2446